TER

stars are handy things, you know. have to do is consult them about a problem — and that's it solved! If, tance, you'd like to impress a new friend by having a special meal — simply find out their star sign.

In our special Jackie guide you'll find all you need to make a hit!

CANCER
(June 21-July 21)

Thrift is the characteristic of the Cancerian — who knows just how to make the pennies stretch. With the help of her powerful imagination she'll be able to make a great meal from next to nothing. You like cooking cheap, tasty meals already, and probably cook quite often for the family. But you're untidy and messy, so the kitchen usually looks like a disaster area by the time you're finished!

You don't worry about your health and weight but you should, as you've always got room for another mouthful and you'll soon pile extra pounds on. A happy home life with the family is something you love, but you need to get out and take fresh air and use up those calories.

BLOW-OUT MEAL
Irish stew

Get scrag end of neck (mutton) from the butcher.
Trim the fat off, place alternate layers of meat and potatoes, onions and parsley in a pan, finishing with a layer of potatoes.
Add water to half cover.
Simmer slowly for three hours.

LEO
(July 22-Aug. 21)

The typical Leo likes to be the centre of attraction at any gathering. So any meal you prepare has to look really good (preferably spectacular). You like doing things in a big way, so cooking a meal is an excellent way to show off. You're a bit of a snob, really, and you'll turn your nose up at ordinary, everyday food.

Being overweight could well be a problem for you, in that everything has to be big and showy — including your helpings! You're a good organiser, so a buffet you'd prepared for your own party would be something else.

You're creative and generous, so cost would be no problem — you'd save up for ages to make a meal to remember.

BLOW-OUT MEAL
Chicken Maryland

Coat chicken portions with seasoned flour, dip in beaten egg and coat with breadcrumbs.
Fry the chicken in butter and oil in a large frying pan until browned.
Turn down heat and cook for twenty minutes.
Serve on a big plate, garnished with fried bananas and fresh watercress.

VIRGO
(Aug. 22-Sept. 21)

You're a hard worker, and rather finicky, which means you can spend hours adding extra, finishing touches to a meal. But you're so fussy and such a worrier that you will only really relax in a restaurant which is *spotlessly* clean. The thought of Sweaty Betty's chipper down the road gives you the horrors!

You're modest, too, so you'd probably prepare a simple but attractive meal for your boyfriend or friends. Weight's not a problem with you because you pick at your food — not that you don't *like* it — you're just that fussy, nibbly little sort of person.

Food's not a major issue in your life, but you'll make an effort if need be.

BLOW-OUT MEAL
Fondue

Rub the inside of a flame-proof dish with a clove of garlic, place over gentle heat and heat ¼ pint dry white wine and lemon juice (a squeeze) in it.
Add 8 oz. Gruyere cheese and stir till melted.
Add two level teaspoonfuls cornflour, pepper, grated nutmeg, and cook further two minutes, till thick and creamy.
To serve, provide cubes of crusty bread which are speared on a fork and dipped in the fondue.
(You can use cider and Cheddar cheese, if preferred.)

For more Star-ters, turn to page 94.

£1·70

CONTENTS

Hello! And welcome to your Jackie Annual 1982! There's loads of goodies in this year's annual (as usual!). There's all your favourites plus lots more surprises. So enjoy your annual, have a great Christmas and don't forget we're around in Jackie every week to make 1982 even more special!
Love,
The Ed.

FICTION

I Tried To Change Him 10
I Saw Him First! 20
It'll Be Better This Time . . . 34
You'll Meet The Right Boy One Day . . . 46
No Place For Love . . . 54
Leonard J. Watkins 82

LIVING

Who's A Pretty Boy, Then? 42

I Only Wanted To Belong 44
How to Handle Him . . . 48
I Was Terrified Of Losing Him . . . 50
The Boy Facts! 76

QUIZZES

Are You A Wonder Woman? 8
Are You A New Romantic? 24
What Goes On In Your Mind? 68

FEATURES

T Time! 15
Ears To You! 22
Getting Fruity! 43
Face The Facts! 61
The Do's and Don'ts of Babysitting! 64

Patchwork 65
Chest A Minute! 66
Make Room For This! 78
Your Dotty Dreams And What They Mean! 81
Do You Know When To Take A Hint? 89

POP

Something Old . . . Something New . . . 6
The Other Dallas Stars . . . 27
Look Who's Talking! 49
How Would You Spend A Winter Evening? 53

Your Jackie Pop-A-Cross 60

Desert Island Delights 63
Playing Around! 74
Something Borrowed . . . Something Blue 90

BEAUTY

Making Faces! 27

ASTROLOGY

For Star-ters! 2

FUN

50 Ways To Keep Smiling! 5
How To Cheer Yourself Up! 16
Boy Talk 17
Is Your Boy The Town Clown? 33
Madge And Beryl 80

You Know You've Got A Lot To Learn When . . . 92

FASHION

Ears To It! 18
Mini-Madness! 26
New Looks 70

50 WAYS TO KEEP SMILING!

1. Keep your savings in your umbrella, so when you open it . . . bingo! You've got the rainy day *and* the money to spend on it.

2. Tell yourself some jokes, and if you run out make them up!

3. Keep a Frown Box — penalty 10p. Even if you lose out at first — you'll smile when opening time comes . . .

4. Make someone happy at least once a day — it's infectious!

5. Tape "The Laughing Policeman" and listen to it once a day, and three times on wet Sundays.

6. Try describing episodes of "The Goodies" to your French pen-friend.

7. Get your dad to replace your ordinary front door with a revolving one, then make sure you're around when the men try to bring in the new carpet . . .

8. Fasten the corners of your mouth up with sticky tape.

9. Sew feathers onto all your garments — to create ar-tickles of clothing!

10. Change your name to Mona Lisa.

11. Buy a kitten and call it "Smiling"!

12. Bet your friends that they can't make you laugh.

13. Wake up thinking about all the lovely things that could happen today — and fall asleep thinking about all the disastrous things that didn't happen.

14. Pose for a photo and try to keep your face straight.

15. Read through the schoolwork you did back in primary school.

16. Enter a sponsored grin.

17. At least once a week do something just for a giggle.

18. Bear in mind that "when you're smiling, the whole world smiles with you" — and you can't top that for majority support!

19. Use eye-shadow in place of lipstick — haven't you ever heard of "The Shadow of Your Smile"?

20. Eat a banana — sideways!

21. Borrow an old kitbag and pack up your troubles in it.

22. Team up with a rich, handsome, kind, generous guy who can't stand to have miserable people around . . .

23. Use your imagination to haul you up when you're down; think of funny things like Barbara Woodhouse trying to train Spit the Dog . . .

24. Paper your bedroom walls with Madge and Beryl strips.

25. Fill your perfume spray with laughing gas.

26. Wander around all day saying, "Cheeeeeeeeeeeese!"

27. Paint a grin on your face.

28. Remember that it takes eighteen muscles to frown and only two to smile — so why work harder than you have to?!

29. Get a job in a joke shop.

30. Sing "Happiness, happiness — the greatest gift that I possess!" at the top of your voice, whenever you're standing in a bus queue in the pouring rain — then enjoy the expressions on the faces of those around you.

31. Offer your boyfriend a kiss for every time he can make you smile . . .

32. Stop watching "Crossroads."

33. Never read any newspaper that's less than a week old, so the horrid events are over by the time you find out about them.

34. Remember that your school days are the happiest days of your life. (If that doesn't cause you to fall about laughing then nothing will!)

35. Switch the telly off whenever a party political broadcast comes on — they only make you hysterical!

36. Make sure there's at least one boy on the bus each morning who'll give you a smile — just in case you forget and leave yours at home.

37. Fit an audi-electronic lock on the biscuit tin — one that only reacts to the sound of your chuckle.

38. Paint the town red regularly, it keeps the blues at bay.

39. Sell all your kid brother's messy paintings as "superb examples of modern art" — and laugh all the way to the bank.

40. Persuade your boyfriend to try to beat the world record for throwing-an-egg-and-catching-it-without-it-going . . . SPLATT!

41. Never worry today about things you can worry about next week — with a bit of luck you'll never remember any of them.

42. Throw away all your sad, soppy records and listen to Madness and Bad Manners all day.

43. Have an uncle called Eric Morecambe.

44. Have a loony friend who always makes you laugh.

45. Every time you're sad, walk on your hands so that at least it *looks* as if you're grinning!

46. Think of Sting!

47. Wear nothing but a smile — so you've *got* to keep that on!

48. Take care of your teeth so that they're so wonderful you'll want to show them off all the time!

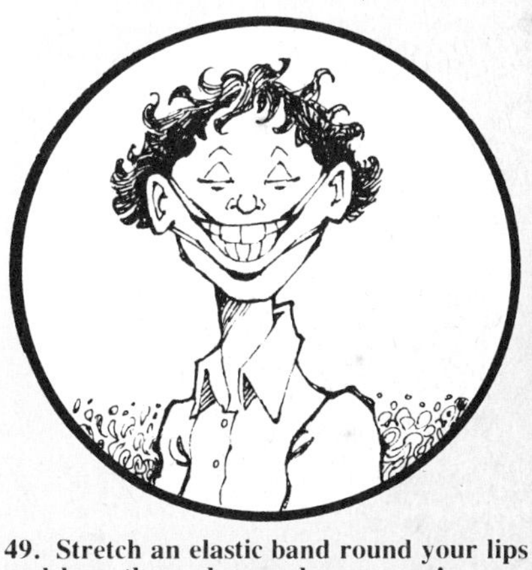

49. Stretch an elastic band round your lips and loop the ends round your ears!

50. Take out a 100-year subscription to Jackie.

SOMETHING OLD...

It's always fun to look back on what's been happening on the music scene at this time of the year.
We've taken a light-hearted look at 1981 and selected some famous faces you're sure to recognise. For some of them it's been business as usual as they produce hit after hit, there's also some bright new talent around, some stars who have cheated a little and "borrowed" ideas from other performers, and some who sadly haven't made it at all this year.
See if you agree!

STATUS QUO. Not one golden oldie here, but four! And really they don't look at all that different now than when they exploded onto the charts with a song called "Pictures Of Matchstick Men" in 1968.

So, Status Quo not only have the privilege of being among the top hit-making bands, but also one of the longest running. Francis Rossi and Alan Lancaster have been playing together since 1962, but it wasn't till Rick Parfitt joined the group six years later that things really started to happen for them.

Perhaps this was just a coincidence . . .

CLIFF RICHARD. None of you, or none of us for that matter, are old enough to remember Cliff when he had his first hit in 1958 with a song called "Move It!" It got to number 3 in the charts and stayed around for eleven weeks.

The rest, as they say, is history and not a year goes by without Cliff hitting the headlines.

No-one would deny him the success he's achieved and you can't help but admire the way his music appeals to all age groups.

What we'd like to know is, how he manages to stay so young-looking. Does he know something we don't know?

PAUL McCARTNEY. Most people are well informed about Paul's vastly famous career from the Beatles' first hit "Love Me Do" in 1962 right up to this day with his super group Wings.

Paul seems to have the Midas touch and like Cliff Richard he seems to get even better looking as he gets older!

Apart from being a brilliant singer/songwriter, he's a great solo performer, businessman and, according to his family, a really super dad.

Some people have all the luck!

DIANA ROSS. For a lady who has an almost grown-up family, Diana isn't doing too badly. Apart from a short spell when she didn't reign "supreme," she's been topping the charts consistently since her first hit with the Supremes in 1967 with a song called "Reflections."

When she realised that disco music was making some people very rich, Diana claimed that she could, "Do that stuff with my eyes shut." She did, and proved that there's still a lot to come from this super singer.

SOMETHING NEW...

ORCHESTRAL MANOEUVRES IN THE DARK. Paul and Andy of OMITD have succeeded in bringing synth music to the fore as an intelligent, lyrical, real form of music.

They've taken care to ensure that it's their music people associate with them and not some clockwork dummy image. So far they've experimented far and beyond other performers working in this field, a move that will guarantee that OMITD will be around for a lot longer than other less creative musicians.

PAULINE MURRAY. Pauline is a lady who's taking on the music scene on her terms. She's successfully created a niche in the market to suit her music and, though her emergence as a solo performer may not have been as explosive as others, she's quietly and confidently built up a strong following.

Her sense of humour is another asset that should stand her in good stead — not many people are zany enough to play with a band called the Invisible Girls who are all males!

STRAY CATS. The runaway success of the crazy-quiffed trio has been quite phenomenal. Long before the band had a hit record or even a recording contract there was an incredible buzz amongst talent scouts, the music press and fellow musicians, about their exciting brand of music.

But they held out till someone offered them a contract with enough money behind it and also one that gave them the opportunity to do things the way they wanted.

The three Americans may not be your idea of the perfect guy but their music is definitely a hit. It's given rockabilly music a whole new sound that isn't steeped in the past but new and very exciting.

ADAM ANT. Adam Ant was just what the doctor ordered last year when he burst on to the pop scene.

Although Adam had been working for a couple of years it wasn't till the original Ants left to join Bow Wow Wow and he formed a new band that he had his first hit with "Dog Eat Dog."

Adam is really a modern-day hero with the looks, talent and image to take the Ants to the top and keep them there. The 80's will surely go down in music history as the years of the Ant!

Now turn to page 90 for Something Borrowed and Something Blue!

A Jackie Quiz

Do TV heroines like Diana Prince and Charlie's Angels make you sick with their daring deeds? Or do you reckon that you could keep up with them without any trouble?

To find out how daring *you* would be in a tricky situation, try our special fun quiz. You'll find out some secrets of your personality, too!

ARE YOU A Wonder Woman?

1. You're walking through a shopping centre when there's a cry of "Stop, thief!" and you see a boy running towards you, hotly pursued. Do you —

a. suddenly remember you wanted something from the shop you're passing, and dive inside,
c. step politely aside to let him through — then trip him up,
b. bring him down with a flying tackle that would make Eddie Waring proud of you,
d. start discussing with the other spectators whether or not he'll be caught?

2. The party is great but nobody's dancing. *You're* just in the mood for some though, so do you —

c. round up a boy and a few friends and get out there to get things going,
a. decide you're too tired for dancing — at least till someone else starts the ball rolling,
d. suggest to the D.J. that he offers a prize that'll soon attract some dancers,
b. grab a boy — and take the opportunity to do your thing and show the others just how it's done?

3. You're sitting alone in the house at night, when suddenly there's a crash of breaking glass somewhere in the vicinity. Do you —

b. grab a torch and go zooming out to investigate,
c. ring your friendly, neighbourhood police station and ask them to investigate,
d. ring your boyfriend, or maybe just the one across the road who smiles at you every morning, and try to get someone to come and investigate,
a. check that the doors and windows are locked and turn the telly up?

4. A man asks you to appear on the local radio station on a panel drawn from the general public. Do you —

a. tell him you're too busy to help out,
b. pinch his clipboard and his pen and write your name in quickly before he changes his mind,
d. ask him what the fee is for appearing, and then make your mind up,
c. ask him what the discussion's about, and go along with it only if it's a subject that interests you?

5. You're on your own at a party but there's a boy who you fancy sitting quietly in a corner looking rather lost. Do you —

c. approach him and start up a conversation,
b. go across, grab him and haul him up to dance,
a. sit nearby, looking equally lost, and hope he'll come across and find you,
d. make a few enquiries to find out why he's on his own — no good getting involved till you've checked him out?

6. Walking home one evening, you hear a plaintive cry from overhead. No, it isn't aliens — it's a cat stuck up a tree. Do you —

a. decide, "You got yourself up there — you can get yourself down!" and carry on walking,
c. try to coax it down — and if that fails coax the fire brigade out to rescue it,

b. shin up the tree like a rocket and bring the poor creature down in triumph,
d. shin a bit of the way up, then look as appealing as the cat sounds and hope someone nice comes and rescues you both?

7. Flicking through the newspaper you see a great job advertised. It looks interesting and exciting, but it would mean moving to a new place. Do you —
b. ring up straight away and make an appointment,
d. draw a ring round the advertisement and leave the newspaper lying around where someone can see it — someone with the power to increase your wages,
a. put off any action until you've had a long think — long enough for you to lose the newspaper,
c. save the cutting — and consider all the angles before you make a move?

8. You wander into the bathroom anticipating a nice, relaxing soak, only to find a huge, great spider sitting in the bath. Do you —
b. pick it up and lob it out the window,
a. decide you're not that dirty, have a fast rinse at the hand-basin and scram,
c. turn on the hot tap and shout "Byeee!" as the intruder whirls away down the plughole,
d. lure it into a jam jar so you can use it to petrify your kid brother, your mum, etc.?

9. A guy you've had your eye on for quite a while suddenly asks you out, but he's offering to take you to some place you've never been before. Do you —
d. feel a bit nervous but reckon it's a good way of finding out what the place is like so you'll know all about it in future,
a. find the combination of new guy and strange place too much and put him off for a while,
c. tell him you'd love to go with him, but to some place you know,
b. find the prospect of new guy and new place quite exhilarating, and accept on the spot?

10. You bought a new dress for a party, but now you find it isn't quite what you expected — there isn't as much of it, for a start! What do you do?
b. Wear it as it is and enjoy causing a sensation.

d. Show it to Dad and see if his indignation will cause him to cough up for something more respectable.
a. Stash it in the wardrobe and wear something else that's not so spectacular.
c. Reduce the length of the slit with a couple of carefully-hidden safety pins?

11. Yippee! You've won first prize in a competition run by a travel agency. You've a choice of prizes, so do you —
d. take a week in some Continental resort where you can laze on the beach, and get a suntan that'll really wow everyone when you get back,
c. take a fortnight in a similar type of resort here in Britain,
b. go for a week to an Alpine resort where you can try things that you haven't tried before — skiing, rock climbing, even breaking a leg,
a. take the money and put it in the bank?

12. Ladders are for window cleaners — not for the new and quite expensive pair of tights you've just taken out of the packet. What are you going to do about this?
b. Charge straight back to the shop and demand to see the manager.
a. Forget it, but don't buy anything from that shop again.
d. Send them back to the manufacturers with a letter of complaint — you might get an apology and a few free pairs!
c. Wander back and talk it over with the shop assistant — and only resort to the manager if you can't get satisfaction.

13. The lift is crowded, in fact, it's a bit too crowded. Halfway up it grinds to a halt. Do you —
c. take command and start buzzing the alarm button,
b. demonstrate your agility by climbing through the escape hatch in the roof, then clambering up to bring help,
a. huddle in a corner and leave it to the others to sort it out, since there's nothing more confusing than everyone talking at once,
d. engage the nearest handsome guy in conversation, since you're going to come out of this eventually you might as well have something to show for it?

Now count your scores, mostly a, b, c, or d, and turn to the conclusions.

Quiz Conclusions

Mostly a.
Shy, hesitant and generally lacking in self-confidence – that's you. It's pretty clear that you're just not at home in any situation which involves an unpredictable element. You're great at coming up with cast-iron reasons why you ***shouldn't*** *do anything that's even slightly risky. Whether it's taking up a new pastime, visiting a new place or accepting a spur-of-the-moment date, you're just not interested.*
Remember though, all things look a bit intimidating at first, but once you've given them a try, you wonder what all the fuss was about. We're not saying you should stick your neck out all the time, but it's certainly time you took your destiny in both hands and applied a little more zest and enthusiasm to your activities.

Mostly b.
Daring, determined and dauntless – you're quite a formidable character. Risks don't bother you in the slightest, in fact, you see them as a challenge, and taking up challenges seems to be your favourite occupation. You're not the type to spend time thinking things over – for you action is called for, and the faster the better! No doubt this characteristic will guarantee you a few spills, but also plenty of thrills, too.
Whilst your very positive personality may put off some of your more timid friends, it's a fair bet they know who to come to when they're facing a crisis. Stay with it, but beware of becoming unsympathetic to those who lack your reckless approach.

Mostly c.
Level-headed, thoughtful and not given to acting on the spur of the moment. If a little daring is required, you have it on tap – but you don't believe in sticking your neck out without good reason. When you take a risk it's one you've considered and calculated first. And if there's an easier way to achieve the end result, you'll find it. Boys probably find you an easy-going and pleasant companion, because you're realistic and not constantly setting them challenges they have to meet.
All in all, you prefer familiar situations to strange ones, but you never shrink from new things when they come up. After all, that's what life's all about!

Mostly d.
Slightly daring you may be – but your real strong point is opportunism! You seem to have the happy knack of turning every risky situation to good use, and manipulating events to provide you with some benefit. You're rather a happy-go-lucky character, and have difficulty in taking anything seriously – even adventures.
Independent, slightly zany, you're always watching for life's little confusions – and using them to gain some advantage over those around you is one of your favourite pastimes. With your qualities you must keep your boys in a state of constant amusement – but keep them you certainly do. On entertainment value alone, you're quite a girl to have around!

I Tried to Change Him

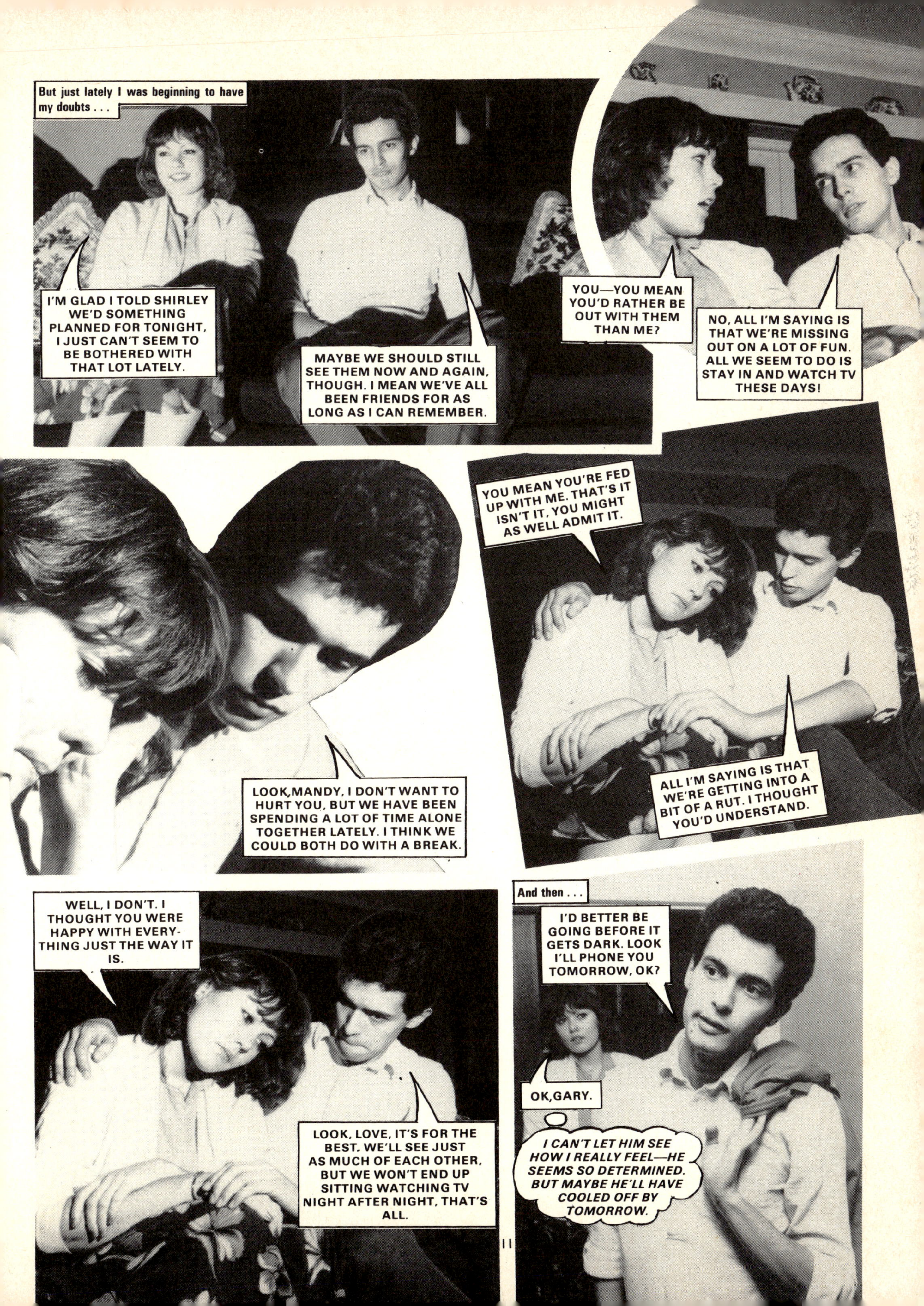
But just lately I was beginning to have my doubts . . .
I'M GLAD I TOLD SHIRLEY WE'D SOMETHING PLANNED FOR TONIGHT, I JUST CAN'T SEEM TO BE BOTHERED WITH THAT LOT LATELY.
MAYBE WE SHOULD STILL SEE THEM NOW AND AGAIN, THOUGH. I MEAN WE'VE ALL BEEN FRIENDS FOR AS LONG AS I CAN REMEMBER.
YOU—YOU MEAN YOU'D RATHER BE OUT WITH THEM THAN ME?
NO, ALL I'M SAYING IS THAT WE'RE MISSING OUT ON A LOT OF FUN. ALL WE SEEM TO DO IS STAY IN AND WATCH TV THESE DAYS!
YOU MEAN YOU'RE FED UP WITH ME. THAT'S IT ISN'T IT, YOU MIGHT AS WELL ADMIT IT.
ALL I'M SAYING IS THAT WE'RE GETTING INTO A BIT OF A RUT. I THOUGHT YOU'D UNDERSTAND.
LOOK,MANDY, I DON'T WANT TO HURT YOU, BUT WE HAVE BEEN SPENDING A LOT OF TIME ALONE TOGETHER LATELY. I THINK WE COULD BOTH DO WITH A BREAK.
WELL, I DON'T. I THOUGHT YOU WERE HAPPY WITH EVERY-THING JUST THE WAY IT IS.
LOOK, LOVE, IT'S FOR THE BEST. WE'LL SEE JUST AS MUCH OF EACH OTHER, BUT WE WON'T END UP SITTING WATCHING TV NIGHT AFTER NIGHT, THAT'S ALL.
And then . . .
I'D BETTER BE GOING BEFORE IT GETS DARK. LOOK I'LL PHONE YOU TOMORROW, OK?
OK,GARY.
I CAN'T LET HIM SEE HOW I REALLY FEEL—HE SEEMS SO DETERMINED. BUT MAYBE HE'LL HAVE COOLED OFF BY TOMORROW.

And so the next night . . .
HI, I'VE GOT GREAT NEWS. MUM'S GONE OUT SO WE'VE GOT THE PLACE TO OURSELVES FOR ONCE!
WELL, I WAS THINKING WE COULD GO DOWN TO THE WIMPY AND MEET UP WITH THE CROWD. BUT IF YOU REALLY DON'T WANT TO . . .
But as the night wore on . . .
YOU'VE BEEN VERY QUIET ALL NIGHT, IS THERE ANYTHING WRONG?
LOOK,MANDY, I'VE EXPLAINED HOW I FEEL, BUT YOU DON'T SEEM TO BE LISTENING TO ME.
ALL I'M SAYING IS THAT I NEED A BIT OF FREEDOM TO DO SOME OF THE THINGS THAT I USED TO—WE BOTH DO!
BUT WE'VE ALWAYS BEEN SO HAPPY. WHAT'S HAPPENED TO CHANGE YOUR MIND?
I—I DON'T KNOW. ALL I DO KNOW IS THAT WE'VE JUST STOPPED HAVING FUN—THAT'S ALL.
I DON'T UNDERSTAND, GARY. I DON'T WANT THINGS TO CHANGE. I'M HAPPY WITH EVERY-THING JUST THE WAY IT IS.
And then . . .
I WAS AFRAID OF THAT. I'M SORRY,MANDY, BUT I JUST DON'T FEEL THE WAY YOU DO. LOOK, I'D BETTER GO. I'LL HAVE TO THINK THINGS OVER. I'LL COME AND SEE YOU TOMORROW SOMETIME.
I'M SORRY,GARY. PLEASE DON'T GO . . .

IT'S NO USE, MANDY. WHY DON'T YOU PHONE ME TOMORROW—MAYBE YOU'LL SEE THINGS DIFFERENTLY IN THE MORNING . . .
I didn't get much sleep that night, but in the morning I'd finally made my decision . . .
THANKS MRS CONWAY, GARY'S PROBABLY ON HIS WAY OVER HERE ANYWAY. NO, IT'S NOT IMPORTANT, BYE!
I'LL GO AND MEET HIM AT THE BUS STOP. SHE SAID HE'D ONLY BEEN GONE FOR ABOUT FIVE MINUTES . . .
But, before I got there . . .
GARY, WHAT ARE YOU DOING HERE? I THOUGHT YOU WERE ON YOUR WAY TO SEE ME!
ER, I'D ARRANGED TO MEET SHIRLEY AND THE OTHERS—WE'RE JUST OFF TO THE PICTURES. NOW THAT YOU'RE HERE, WHY DON'T YOU JOIN US?
YOU—YOU MEAN YOU WERE GOING WITHOUT ME!
WELL, LET'S FACE IT. YOU'RE NOT EXACTLY A BUNDLE OF LAUGHS THESE DAYS. YOU DON'T SEEM TO CARE WHAT I WANT—IT'S GOT TO BE YOUR WAY EVERY TIME.
AND I SUPPOSE FROM NOW ON EVERYTHING'S GOING TO BE SHIRLEY'S WAY!
LOOK,MANDY, WE WERE GOING TO SURPRISE YOU BY DROPPING IN AFTER WE'D BEEN TO THE PICTURES. HONESTLY, THERE'S NOTHING IN IT . . .
WELL,THIS IS ONE SURPRISE YOU'VE HAD COMING FOR A LONG TIME, YOU JEALOUS BITCH—YOU'VE ALWAYS WANTED GARY, HAVEN'T YOU?

And before I could stop myself . . .
DON'T! THERE'S NOTHING BETWEEN GARY AND ME. WE WERE ONLY WORRIED ABOUT YOU!
I just froze afterwards as I watched Gary put his arm round Shirley . . .
ARE YOU OK, SHIRLEY?
COME ON,SHIRL, LET'S GET OUT OF HERE. I'M REALLY SORRY, I'D NO IDEA SHE FELT LIKE THAT ABOUT YOU.
I tried to explain things to Gary, but it was just no good . . .
YOU'RE JUST A SELF-CENTRED BITCH, MANDY. I'VE HAD ENOUGH OF YOUR MOODS AND RUDENESS AND AS FAR AS I'M CONCERNED, I NEVER WANT TO SEE YOU AGAIN!
DON'T SAY THAT, GARY. I ONLY CAME AFTER YOU TODAY TO TELL YOU THAT YOU WERE RIGHT AND THAT I DIDN'T WANT TO LOSE YOU. BUT IT'S TOO LATE AND NOW I'VE LOST EVERYTHING. . .
THE END

There are different ways of crossing a "t" — high up the stem, to the left, to the right, looped or bowed.
Some people may use a few different ways but *everybody* has one they use more than any other — and this one is the most significant.
The way you cross your "t" gives away lots of information. If *you'd* like to know more about yourself (and other people!) cast an eye over the examples we've got here and see what you can find . . .

T time!

The bar of the letter does not go through its stem.
This shows a tendency to be over-cautious and indecisive. There's also a lack of willpower behind any decisions eventually taken.

A weak, sagging bar.
Typically, this would belong to someone who's easily led, and who likes to take the easiest way out.

A t bar which curves back on itself.
This is the mark of a self-centred person who can frequently be very selfish.

A strong, well-balanced t bar, crossing in the middle of the stem.
This shows good control of emotions and a well-balanced, dependable and hard-working person who likes to get things done.

A very low bar.
This bar indicates a very modest nature plus a lack of ambition. This sort of person is perfectly happy doing nothing.

A t bar set high and above the stem.
This belongs to someone who aims high, has lots of imagination, a spirit of adventure and likes to be a perfectionist.

The bar is curved in a bow shape above the stem.
This shows a high degree of control and discipline with a leaning towards interests like the supernatural.

Hooks on the end of the bar.
A strong will and determination is indicated. Someone who is capable of hard work, and one who will see things through to the finish.

too

The bar extends over other letters
This shows a protective streak and a desire to mother, and smother, people.

The bar is thicker at one end, like a club.
A give-way to an unpredictable nature, and a slow temper which is very violent when it does give way!

A t bar slanting upwards.
This indicates ambition, and a desire for self improvement. The owner of this letter is a tip for the top!

A downward pointing bar.
This is a sign of the fighter, a person who is aggressive, stubborn and likes the last word – in everything.

The bar is placed after the stem.
A hasty, animated and enthusiastic person bubbling over with nervous energy. Thoughts tend to run ahead of actions. It may reveal a quick temper if coupled with heavy pressure.

No t bar.
This may be due to carelessness or absentmindedness but it reveals a difficulty in getting things started.

So you've got a thin, weak t bar low down on the stem and you'd put your head in the oven and end it all if only your house wasn't all electric?
Don't despair. All you have to do is change your "t". A firm, mid-placed t bar will make all the difference to your writing, and who knows, your lifestyle may change for the better, too!

HOW TO–
Cheer Yourself Up!

GET YOUR EARS PIERCED

— if you haven't already! Buy the silliest earrings you can find, or design and make your own — you can buy basic kits in the craft shops and some department stores.

GO OUT FOR A CHINESE MEAL

— and try chopsticks! This does wonders for the diet and digestion, as it's practically impossible to lift rice or noodles with two straight, smooth pieces of wood! The trick is to get your face as close to the plate as possible and *shovel*, but by the time you've got the hang of it you'll probably be laughing so much, the whole restaurant will be in an uproar and you'll be escorted firmly to the door and asked not to come back!

VISIT THE LIBRARY

– where there are lots of lovely, untouched males lurking amongst the literature. This type of boy is usually an intellectual, but he'll make a good boyfriend because he's always curious to find out about new and interesting things – like you!

COUNT YOUR FRECKLES

– well, someone might have stolen one!

WEAR A DIFFERENT FACE EVERY DAY OF THE WEEK

Dig out all the eyeshadows and lipsticks which have lain mouldering at the bottom of your make-up bag for months and really go to town! Make yourself up as a Red Indian, a clown or a South Sea Islander, then throw a fancy dress party and award yourself first prize!

TALK TO YOUR GRAN OR GRANDAD ABOUT THEIR CHILDHOOD

Ask them how they used to celebrate Christmas; what school was like; what sort of clothes they wore; how they survived without the telly!; how they met.

If you're feeling particularly energetic, get them to teach you some Old Time dances — you'll need to have a night at the disco for a rest!

THROW OUT YOUR JUNK!

Yes, *all* of it. Even *you* have to admit that things have got a bit out of hand when you walk into your room and you can't find the bed, so get rid of all those holey tights you keep to wear under trousers, and the bits of broken jewellery

you've always meant to mend, and have a good weep over all your old love letters!

Send all your games and books to the local hospital, trundle any still-wearable clothes down to the Oxfam Shop, and present your doctor or dentist with all the magazines you've hoarded since Issue No. 1 — except Jackie, of course . . .

DO YOUR WASHING THE OLD-FASHIONED WAY!

No sudless soap-powder or automatic machines – get your sleeves rolled up, the rubber gloves on and pile in! This may, not ***seem*** *the ideal way to cheer yourself up, but it has hidden advantages – (a) you will have very clean cothes and (b) you will be very popular with your mother.*

START A COLLECTION OF USELESS FACTS

When you're feeling cheesed off, it'll cheer you up no end to know that Louis XIV of France was born with two teeth, or that wallabies breed wild in Derbyshire!

WRITE OFF FOR A PEN PAL — WRITE AWAY!

There are thousands of people all over the world who'd be only too glad to write to you (poor misguided fools!) so send off for addresses through school organisations or look up penpal columns in newspapers and mags and start scribbling!

BOY TALK

Danny's Christmas message to the nation!

WHAT are your plans for Christmas? Lots of parties and lots of fun? Me, too. You hear people saying that Christmas is only for kids.

Are they crazy?

I reckon to have as much fun at Christmas as I did when I was a kid. Of course, I don't find a Rupert or a Beano Annual in my stocking any more.

I did hang up a stocking last year, just in case, but my flat mate, Steve, filled it up with jelly. Imagine plunging your hand into a nice full stocking in the early hours of Christmas morning and finding nothing but cold squidgy jelly. It was horrible!

IT pays to be extra nice to all your friends in the weeks before Christmas. That way they're likely to remember you when they're wondering who to invite to their parties.

Last year I got invited to so many parties I didn't have time to throw one of my own — so I paid them all back by having a Christmas party in April.

Steve and I are giving a party at our place this Christmas. We're calling it a Hallowe'en party.

We've invited more girls than boys, because we're greedy, but Steve turned down my great idea of inviting all girls.

"We've got to have some time off to eat and drink," he said. "All that kissing and cuddling makes you hungry." Speak for yourself, Steve . . .

I've been to one pre-Christmas party already, at Carol's hospital.

I even danced with the matron. I didn't mean to, I was only trying to get past her to go to the nosh counter but she got the wrong idea.

I had to sit down for a little while afterwards but I soon felt better when I found I was sitting under the mistletoe.

It's not every guy who can claim to have been kissed by almost the entire female staff of a large hospital. When they'd all finished I had to go down to the Casualty Department to have my lips un-puckered.

CHRISTMAS is a terrific time to make new friends. Everybody's relaxed and happy and even if you're a bit shy you find it a lot easier to join in.

I hope you've got a nice guy of your very own to share Christmas with, but if you haven't, this is your chance to meet one. Most guys, like me, need an excuse to get to know a girl. If she looks friendly and there's a bunch of mistletoe nearby — he's in business.

Or if she's loaded down with Christmas shopping, and looking like she's not going to make it home, he's going to grab the opportunity.

I know what I'm talking about. How do you think I met most of my girlfriends?

Happy Christmas. And have a really great New Year, won't you?

Love,

Danny x

EARS TO IT!

You don't have to spend pounds on earrings — with a bit of imagination you only need to spend a few pence — if you make your own!

Pale purple sea shell.

Cocktail parasol with raffia attached.

Christmas tree bauble.

Earrings are very popular just now, with more and more people getting their ears pierced – often two or three times.

The jewellery stands in shops offer an enormous range of sparkly, brightly coloured things to hang from your lobes – many of which seem to be a bit too expensive for what they are, especially if you're prone to losing them!

This year, we've seen a lot of huge, brassy dangling earrings around, which have an ethnic African or Egyptian influence – but anything goes – as long as it's large!

It's very easy and cheap to make your own earrings and the great thing about it is that they'll be unique – you're not likely to see everyone else wearing a pair exactly the same as yours, which is another problem with shop-bought earrings.

Once you start thinking about making your own earrings – the possibilities are endless!

Curtain rings, old necklaces, wooden beads, toys, buttons, are just a few of the things you could use. Even those tiny plastic toys you get inside crackers would make great earrings.

Have a look round the house – there are bound to be hundreds of things you could use!

The earrings shown here were all made from collected objects with the help of a strong glue and the odd coating of enamel paint. They're the handiwork of Deborah Allison, a first year fashion student at Ravensbourne College of Art and Design.

"I started to make earrings because a lot of the ones on the market were too expensive and not individual enough," Deborah told us. "At one time I had as many as fifty different earrings, made from anything I could get my hands on – like marbles, coloured paper clips, and fuses in different colours.

"The good thing about them is that they're just for fun and they don't cost anything, so it doesn't matter if you lose them, as earrings do tend to drop off very easily."

Earring Aids:

If you're interested in making yourself some earrings, the clips can be bought from craft shops, bead shops and street market stalls, or you could send for them. Creative Bead Craft Ltd., Unit 26, Chiltern Trading Estate, Earl Howe Road, Holmer Green, High Wycombe, Bucks., do a small order service, and have a wide selection of beads and earrings clips. Write to them for details, enclosing a stamped addressed envelope.

Remember – don't wear anything too large, heavy or breakable on your ears!

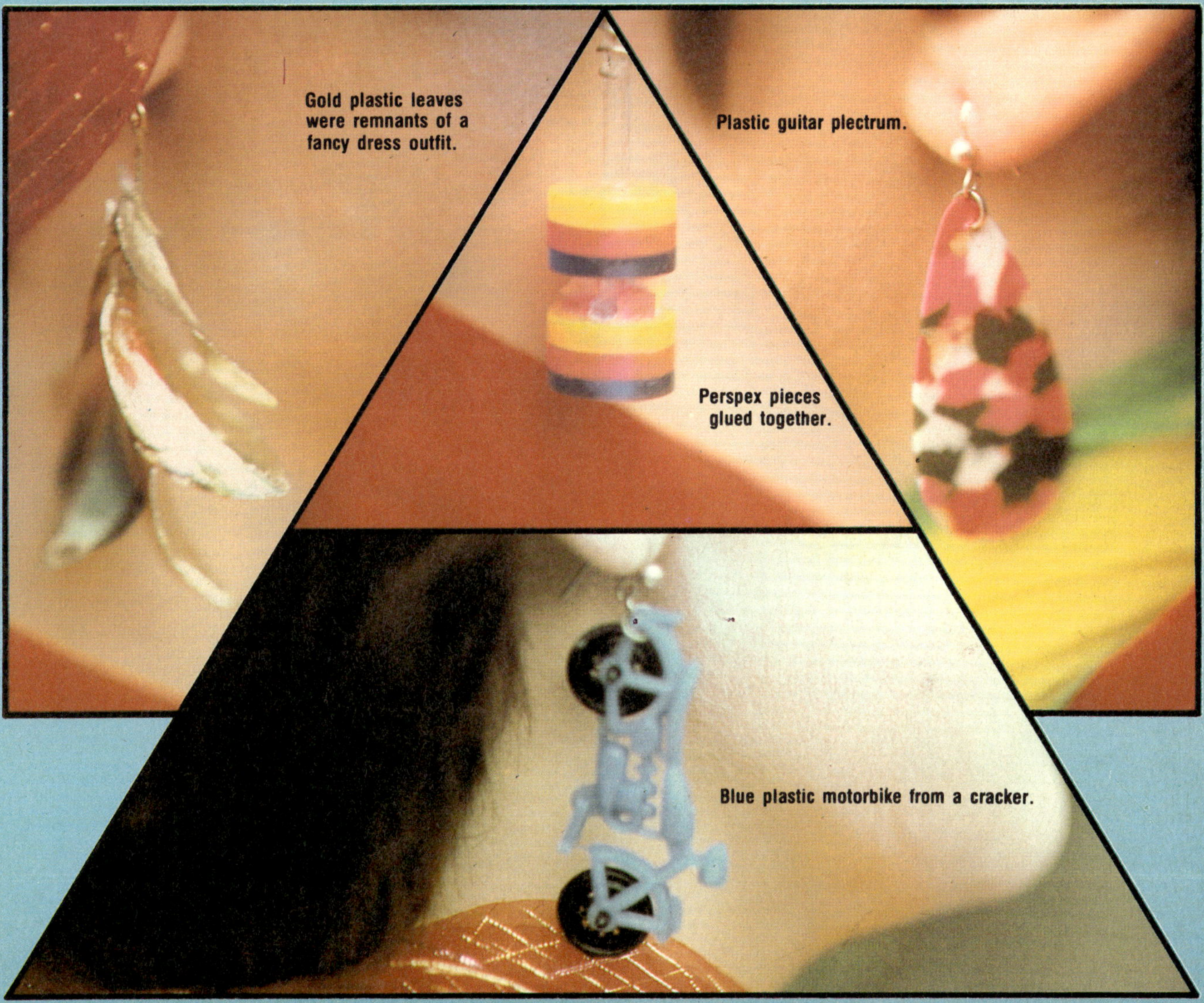

I SAW HIM FIRST!

HIS name was Paul and he was gorgeous. Everyone thought so – especially me. Naturally, I fancied him like mad – everyone did! – but just for once, I seemed to have the advantage over all my giggling rivals.

*I had discovered, by means of a great deal of effort and a bit of very unsubtle detective work, that Paul lived just three streets away from me **and** that we went to the same school, although he was in a different form. There was, however, a Snag.*

Martine. Actually, she was (occasionally) my friend, but not so's you'd notice. Not that you could help noticing Martine, with her glossy black hair, glossy red lips and glossy-magazine clothes.

She also lived near Paul and went to the same school, and I lived in constant fear of the moment that he would notice her and be helplessly dazzled.

*I would never, ever have wanted Paul to **know** that I was chasing him, of course – a girl has her pride. But I certainly wasn't going to let that female piranha have him without putting up a bit of a fight . . .*

So, on a rather nice, crisp winter morning, I decided to begin "Operation Paul." I knew (because of all the time I'd spent snooping around) exactly when he was due to walk past the end of my street, so I dawdled along as slowly as I could, praying that Martine wouldn't arrive at the same time.

About five minutes later, after I'd looked at everything I could possibly look at, then examined it in minute detail again, Paul appeared.

I pretended to be very interested in

*Paul just gaped after her and I sagged inwardly. I was no competition **at all** after that little display.*

"Well," I said, with a light laugh. "Back to the grind!"

"Mmm . . ." said Paul, in a very absent-minded voice. I gave up. He would never be mine.

BY the end of the day, of course, I had recovered a bit, and decided to have another go. Maybe I wasn't as devastating as Martine, but I wasn't bad. Mum was always telling me I was quite pretty.

It did bother me a bit, though, that mothers tend to say that even if their child has a face that would frighten a horse . . . But I put that disturbing thought to the back of my mind and decided to walk home by way of Paul's house.

He'd be almost bound to catch me up, I thought, so I wandered along quite slowly.

He didn't, of course, and I was back in the dumps again before I got to my own front door. Martine must have caught him, I thought miserably, and he's so besotted, he hasn't the strength to resist.

*Next morning, though, **he** was hanging around on **my** street corner, just for a change. As I walked towards him, trying to look cool and unconcerned, he smiled straight at me and I felt myself flush scarlet all over.*

He looked so gorgeous that it took me a few minutes to realise he was actually speaking to me.

" . . . Adam and the Ants con-

she breathed, "but of course, it was twice as nice meeting you and Ron there . . ."

What you might term a faint glimmer of hope began to flicker through my deepest, darkest despair. She and Paul hadn't met on purpose and they hadn't been alone . . .

" . . . he did suggest that we should get Rona to make up a four one night." She paused for effect. "Could be fun," she purred, batting her eyelashes.

Paul looked up, rather enthusiastically, I thought. I wanted to die right on the spot.

"That would be great!" he said. "I sort of suspected you were quite keen on Ron! And if Rona'll come with me, we can definitely get something organised!"

THE world spun round and Martine seemed to disappear. When the world stopped spinning round, she appeared again, looking red and angry and deflated and blazing mad! She didn't make a fool of herself by explaining that he'd got it all wrong, though.

She was far too sophisticated and cool for that and she wasn't going to ruin her image, even for Paul . . .

I became vaguely aware that Paul was speaking to me. "That is, if you don't mind, Rona?"

I hesitated exactly two seconds. "It sounds smashing to me!" I said, grinning all over my face.

He moved a little closer. Not so close that it made much difference, but still . . .

I turned to Martine and said, "Thanks," she said, stiffly. "I'll think about it and let you know."

She smiled as if the effort would kill her and stalked off as soon as we got to the school gates.

Once we were alone, I heard Paul take a deep breath and say, "Great girl, Martine. She must've known that I've been wanting to get to know you for ages. It was nice of her to arrange all this.

*"Mind you –" He looked at the ground, and coughed slightly. "She can be a bit **overpowering**, can't she?"*

I choked, and he had to slap me on the back before I recovered enough to walk into class. What a good thing, I thought, as he put his arm round me, that some of us were more – subtle about things . . .

A Jackie short story specially written by Winnie Czulinski.

I'd fancied Paul for ages — but so had Martine. And what chance did I have against Westdale School's answer to Debbie Harry . . .?

two horrible little boys having a snowball fight on the other side of the road and waited until he called out to me before I looked round.

"Rona! Rona, wait a minute!"

Gratified, I turned and watched him squelch up to me. His voice made my blood run sort of hot and cold at the same time, but, of course, I wasn't going to let him know that.

"Hello," I said, as calmly as I could.

"Hello, Paul," said Martine, appearing as if by magic from a side-street.

PAUL turned. "Oh – Martine! I didn't expect to see you this early!"

"No," I said, gritting my teeth. "Nor did I!"

She ignored me. "You're looking good this morning, Paul," she murmured, batting her eyelashes. Paul blushed.

"Er – thanks, Martine. Why don't you walk along with us?" he said, like the gentleman he is.

Why he had to choose that particular moment to be a gentleman, I don't know, but we walked along together – in total silence. I thought the sultry looks Martine was casting at Paul would melt the snow and I spent the rest of the walk dreaming up terrible things that could happen to her between here and the school gates.

"Well," she breathed as we reached the playground, "simply must dash to – biology!" She ran her eyes over Paul as if she would have just loved to experiment on him and wiggled off.

"I was thinking of going to the Odeon – there's a good film on – or the Palais – there's a concert . . ." he was saying. "I was thinking –"

"Yes?" said Martine, sidling up from somewhere behind him and planting herself very deliberately between us.

I closed my eyes and thought very uncharitable thoughts, about how many years I'd get in jail for strangling someone with their own scarf. When I opened them, she had put her arm through Paul's. She smiled at me, smugly.

"Paul was telling you about the wonderful time we had last night, was he? I can't remember when I enjoyed myself so much!"

I FELT my mouth open and I shut it sharpish, feeling more of a fool than I could bear. What wonderful time? When? Where? I thought desperately. To add insult to injury, I also dropped all my books (from shock) and had to get down on my hands and knees to gather all the bits and pieces together.

I must have looked really awkward, scrambling about in the snow while the immaculate Martine looked on, sneering faintly.

"Here, Rona," Paul was saying. "Let me give you a hand."

I collected my books and what remained of my dignity, thanked Paul as graciously as I could, and the three of us walked along together.

At least, Paul and Martine were together – I was relegated to the iciest area on the outside of the pavement.

Paul was looking a bit pink for some reason and he didn't seem to want to look at Martine. It was so obvious he was really keen on her – boys are like that . . .

She didn't give **me** *a look in, of course – she kept talking all the way along the road.*

"I always did like the coffee bar," innocently, "Where do you think Ron would like to go? All this was your idea, so it's only fair that you should choose!"

JEWELLERY IS VERY INDIVIDUAL. IT'S A MATTER OF TASTE, SO YOUR CHOICE IS BOUND TO REVEAL SOMETHING ABOUT YOUR PERSONALITY. SO WITH THAT IN MIND, DARE YOU READ OUR FEATURE ABOUT EARRINGS? IF ALL THIS MAKES YOU FEEL LIKE RUSHING OUT AND BUYING A BALACLAVA TO HIDE BEHIND, THOUGH — DON'T. *YOU* MAY BE BARING ALL — BUT THEN SO IS EVERYONE ELSE! SO IF YOU WANT TO BECOME AN EXPERT AT CHARACTER ANALYSIS, READ ON!

EARS TO YOU!

PLASTIC EARRINGS

This girl likes a lot for her money. She lives life to the full, and enjoys every minute of it. She has a great personality and is always fun to have around. Not content to follow the crowd, she has her own ideas and is prepared to defend them. She likes to be noticed and with her zany dress sense, she always is.

She has an easy come, easy go personality, and never takes anything too seriously. She's a bit of a trendsetter, and is always way ahead of everyone else where fashion is concerned, but ideas and crazes don't last long with her. She soon gets bored with them and flits on to something else. Nothing in her life is permanent, everything is disposable — including boyfriends! The plastic earring wearer does not give her heart forever, only lends it for a while. She enjoys doing the chasing, as well as being chased, but tends to lose interest very quickly once she's actually caught him. Because of this free and easy attitude to relationships, she is labelled a flirt, which is rather unfair — she's just naturally very friendly.

SEVERAL ASSORTED EARRINGS IN ONE EAR

The girl who wears several earrings in each ear is a dizzy girl, full of fun and once she starts giggling, there's just no stopping her. She's also rather giddy and never thinks before she acts, consequently landing herself in all sorts of scrapes. She can be rather careless, but she really doesn't mean any harm — it's just that she really didn't *think*. And that just about sums up her whole attitude to life — bright and breezy, living for today without a thought for the future.

Although she is fun to be with, she doesn't make lasting friendships, just lots of casual

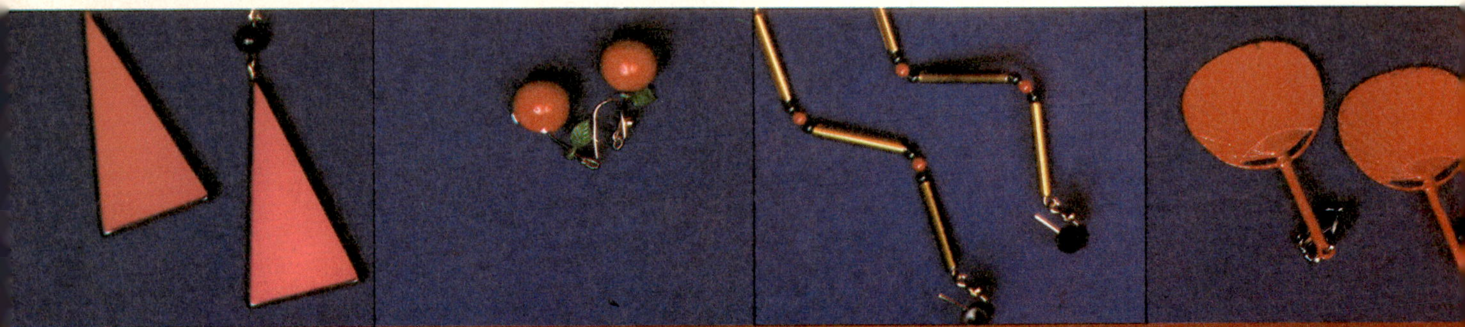

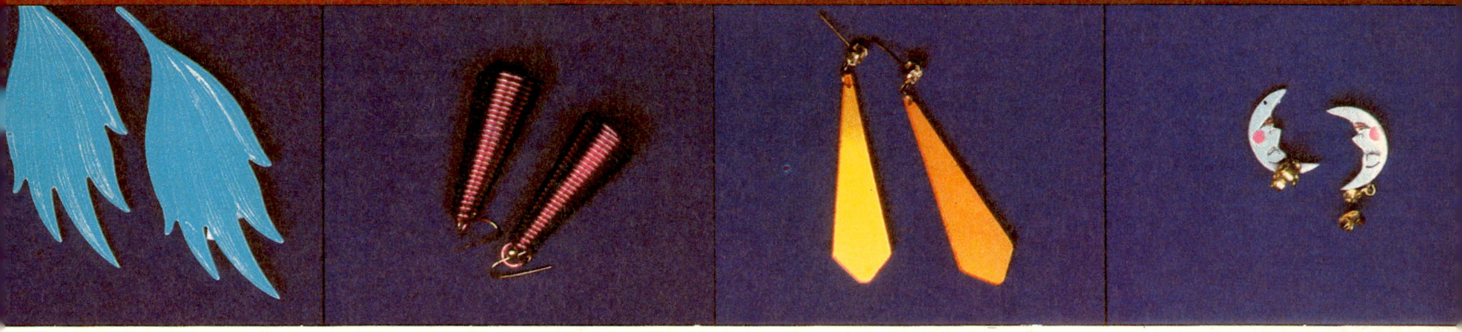

acquaintances. Because she needs to be reassured that she's attractive, she's quite happy to go out with any boy who asks her, seeming not to notice the harm this is doing her reputation. And, of course this behaviour doesn't exactly make her very popular with other girls!

NO EARRINGS

The girl who hasn't had her ears pierced is a bit of a cowardly custard. Timid and shy, she's afraid of trying anything different and is quite content to walk in the shadow of her more daring friends.

She never has a lot to say for herself — it's not that she's dumb, it's just she considers her thoughts too boring to interest anyone else. She rarely lets her emotions show or gets excited about anything, from fear of being laughed at, and because of this, boys often dismiss her as dull and unfriendly.

When she falls for a boy, she falls really hard and is so willing to please, she'll always do as he wishes and is prepared to defend him to the last. This also means she'll be very upset when he finishes with her and will think twice before giving her heart again.

Basically, this girl lacks confidence in herself. If only someone would take a real interest in her, she'd soon come out of her shell and show what a super sympathetic and fun friend she'd make.

DIAMANTE DANGLERS

The girl who wears these is a bit like a magpie — she loves collecting bright, flashy things —

especially boys! She relies on her looks to get noticed, and is forever peering into mirrors to see if her hair's alright. All her money goes on clothes, but especially on lots of pretty nick-nacks and jewellery.

Never content with only one guy at a time, she likes to have several fussing and fighting over her as it makes her feel important and wanted. Basically, this girl is insecure. Only by flirting with every guy in sight does she get the attention she craves.

The sad thing is, deep down she longs for a steady relationship and since she regards her flirting as harmless fun, she can't understand why others get so upset about it.

GOLD SLEEPERS

The girl who wears gold sleepers has more than a bit of gipsy in her soul. She's a rebel by nature and hates being told what to do. She has a fiery temperament and is a wildly exciting, passionate girl. She never does anything by half, committing herself completely to whatever she's doing. The problem is, she tends to lose interest very quickly, and rarely finishes what she starts.

She demands unquestioning devotion from friends and boyfriends and tends to surround herself with people who will bow to her wishes and obey her every command, although secretly she despises such weak-willed characters.

Basically, she is very moody, with a fiery temper, and boy, do sparks fly when she loses it — which she does at least every few hours.

Boys find her fiery nature very attractive at first and feel proud to have won her, but they soon realise she's not such a great prize and tire of her jealousy and nagging ways. Even if he is prepared to put up with her moods, she'll soon get bored with him, and dull routine is something she is not prepared to put up with.

STUDS

This girl is practical and sensible, with her feet planted firmly on the ground. She's a career girl, and has her sights fixed on the top and has the drive and ability to get there. She's willing to work and study hard to get on in the world. However, this doesn't mean she doesn't know how to enjoy herself — she does, but not when it interferes with her work.

She knows exactly where she's going and plans her life down to the smallest detail. Precise and neat, she can't abide carelessness or thoughtlessness of any kind, and lateness is something which really annoys her.

Boys, however, tend to be rather scared of her, thinking her too good for them, with all those qualifications and certificates. She, in turn, regards boys of her own age as silly and childish, and longs for someone older and more sensible to whom she can relate.

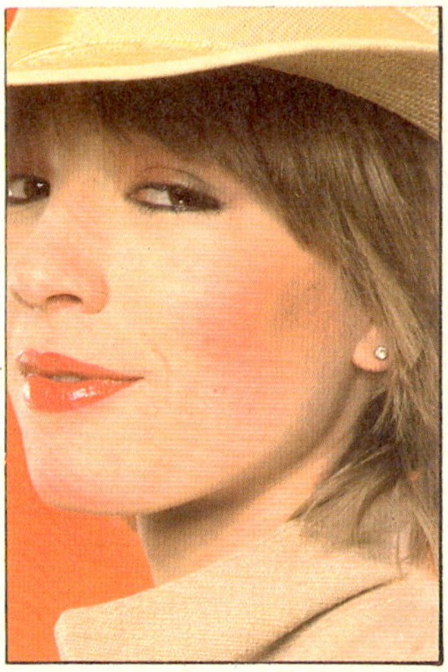

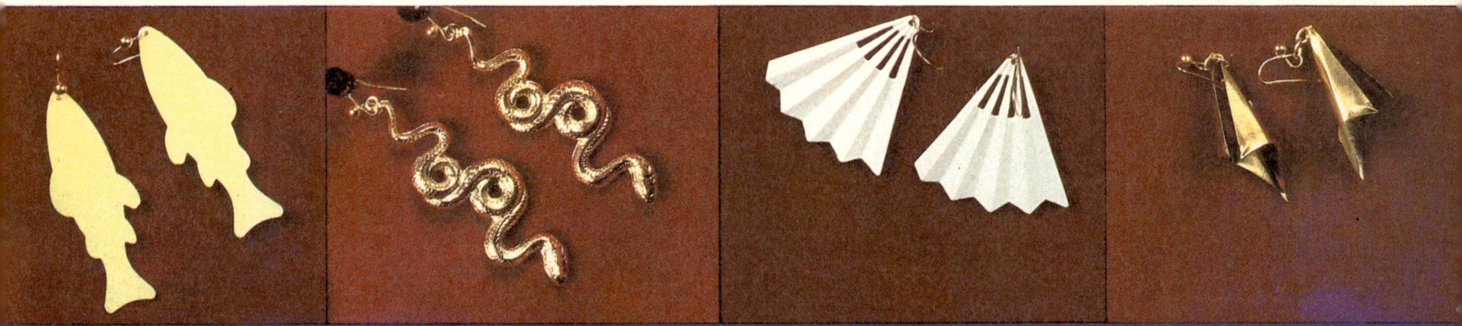

Are You A New Romantic?

Romance means more than the moon in June and a handsome Spanish waiter, you know — there's a whole romantic world waiting out there for you . . . if you can drag yourself away from "Crossroads" and your mum's steak-and-kidney pie. Do you have that romantic streak that transforms the ordinary — or would you have difficulty recognising romance if it was handed to you on a plate garnished with roses? Our quiz tests how romantic you are — and you might discover a more mysterious side to your personality!

Look at the pictures below and, before reading the questions, try to decide your own immediate response to them – for instance, do they bore you? Or make you recall the past, or fire your imagination? It may be difficult at first, so perhaps you could scribble your reactions down on a separate sheet of paper, then try to match them up with our interpretations . . .

1. Do you:
a. think: Yuck! It looks like boring old Beethoven!
b. suddenly hear a snatch of your favourite music,
c. wish you could read music,
d. conjure up a picture of a string quartet, sitting amidst the potted palms in some luxurious hotel,
e. go into raptures – you've always had a great love of classical music?

2. Do you:
a. feel uninterested – it looks very old fashioned,
b. imagine your boyfriend Bill kissing ***you,***
c. recognise the actors as two lesser-known Hungarians and put a name to a very obscure movie,
d. think: It's the latest big-star film – "Son Of Love Story!" I must go and see it tonight,
e. remember with a pang of melancholy how fleeting human love is . . .?

3. Do you:
a. shudder at the thought of all the worms and creepy-crawlies that probably live around there,
b. think it looks a good place for a picnic with all your friends,
c. think it looks a rotten place for a picnic because the grass is too long to sit on comfortably,
d. it bores you – it just comes over as rather damp and dull,
e. feel the tree is strangely evil, compared to the sunny field beyond?

4. Do you:

a. consider the girl is taking a stupid risk by not wearing a helmet,
b. think: I bet they don't know where they're heading – and that's the best part of it,
c. envy them their freedom and wish you were the girl on the back,
d. admit that it looks fun, but feel they're wasting energy and polluting the environment,
e. hate going fast but suppose you'd ride if someone offered?

5. Do you:

a. wish you were a little girl again,
b. have no opinion about it – you don't really see what's happening in this picture,
c. think the dog looks as though he's going to bite the child,
d. think it's a really sweet picture – the little boy's adorable,
e. wonder what the little boy has been saying to the dog?

Now go through your answers, checking them against the list below and add up your points total before reading our down-to-earth conclusions on your romantic rating!

1. a-3, b-1, c-4, d-2, e-5.
2. a-3, b-4, c-2, d-5, e-1.
3. a-5, b-2, c-4, d-3, e-1.
4. a-4, b-1, c-5, d-2, e-3.
5. a-2, b-3, c-4, d-5, e-1.

QUIZ CONCLUSIONS:

IF YOU SCORED:

6 or under: You show signs of possessing the true romantic spirit — basically you're a person for whom the inner world of the imagination is more important, yet you're intensely aware of the natural world. You've a strong urge to express yourself artistically, but your creativity is also apparent in your endless search for love and adventure.

You often feel alienated from other people and depressed by the triviality of daily life. You long to escape this by travel and are fascinated by foreign lands, and you would go anywhere, do anything, for ideals that you believe in. You can be rather selfish and treat your friends and family off-handedly sometimes. You'll be sure to amaze everyone some day — but remember not to cut yourself off from human companionship — loneliness is not the same as solitude.

7-11: You're more a true friend to romantics than one yourself. You admire them for their spiritual qualities and soaring imaginations — but don't under-estimate yourself. You've a pretty strong imagination yourself, and probably spend a good deal of your time day-dreaming. You're good at learning and are knowledgeable about books, drama and music, though your interest is perhaps more passive than active.

You never find life boring — you're prepared to take an interest in everyone and everything (in fact, we bet you enjoy a good gossip!) and have loads of loyal friends and an active social life. You're aware of your responsibilities as a member of society, and with your mixture of realism and idealism, you're good at arguing a point — and could well end up in the politics! Be careful, though, to develop your own opinions or you might end up as a yes-woman!

12-16: You're probably at the stage when your personality is still developing and your experience of the world is fairly limited. You tend to be a bit scared of the unknown, although you wouldn't mind adventure if the whole gang went along!

You wouldn't win any prizes for being observant but you're vaguely aware that you're not living life to the full; you'd find things a lot more interesting if you made an effort to get involved in some activities that would drag you away from the telly! You can't rush experience, but staying in a rut is all too comfortable for someone as easy-going as you . . .

17-21: You're the practical one — but we need people like you to run the world, so don't feel you're missing out on things. In fact, you're very attached to everyday things and your home is very important to you, although your concern with possessions could turn into snobbishness. You get on well with your parents, and if you've younger brothers and sisters you'll naturally accept responsibility for them.

When it comes to love you may well marry young, and loyalty and fidelity are essential to your peace of mind. You hate pretence and irresponsibility of any kind (ideal school prefect material!) so you tend to judge people very quickly — and usually correctly. However, you *can* make mistakes when it comes to more unconventional people, so try to develop a little more tolerance.

22-25: You're a sentimentalist rather than a romantic — you don't really feel as deeply as you make out and people may see you as a bit of a poser. You probably feel fairly insecure about your position and personality and think that the *real* you is rather dull and uninteresting. You like to keep up with the latest fashion and beauty trends but your knowledge of anything else is rather superficial and patchy — which only adds to your feelings of insecurity.

You're a worrier and suffer badly from nerves, but you should confess your anxieties to a good friend and stop trying to live up to a false image — and remember to choose as friends girls you really like, rather than those you think are the in-crowd. If you've always had a secret desire to write a book entitled "100 Ways With Turnips" then just go ahead and do it! It may not be romantic, but at least it's honest . . .

MINI-MADNESS!

A KNIT-A-BIT PATTERN

This super looking mini-dress, exclusively designed for Jackie readers by Alan Dart, is well worth the time spent knitting it — considering the amount of wear you're going to get out of it!

It'll look good with thick tights and ankle boots or dressed up with flat gold pumps and lots of gold jewellery — or you can cheat a bit and wear it as an over-sized jumper with your jeans!

Whichever way you wear it you can snuggle up with style this winter!

MATERIALS — 16 (17, 17) balls (50 g) of Sirdar Palamino; 2 (2, 2) balls (50 g) of Sirdar Majestic in matching shade.
NEEDLES — A pair each of 4 mm (No. 8) and 6½ mm (No. 3).
MEASUREMENTS — To fit *32 (34, 36) in.* bust; length *31 (32, 33) in.*; sleeve seam *17 in.*
TENSION — 15 sts and 20 rows to 10 cm *(4 in.)* square, measured over stocking-stitch using Palamino on 6½ mm needles.
ABBREVIATIONS — K — knit; P — purl; st, sts — stitch(es); tog — together; beg — beginning; inc — increase by working into front and back of stitch; dec — decrease by working 2 stitches together; comm — commencing, commencement.

NOTE — The purl side of the knitting is used as the right side.

Instructions for larger sizes in brackets.

BACK
With 4 mm needles and Majestic cast on 69 (73, 77) sts and work 20 rows K1, P1 rib.
Change to 6½ mm needles and Palamino and continue in stocking-stitch comm with a P row.
Work 33 (35, 37) rows.
Dec 1 st at beg and end of next row.
Repeat the last 34 (36, 38) rows once more 65 (69, 73) sts
Work 32 (34, 36) rows ending with a K row.
Shape armholes — Cast off 4 sts at beg of next 2 rows 57 (61, 65) sts. *.
Dec 1 st at beg of next and every following row until 51 (53, 55) sts remain.
Continue without shaping until 140 (146, 152) rows Palamino have been worked from comm.
Shape shoulders — Cast off 14 (15, 16) sts at beg of next 2 rows.
Cast off remaining 23 sts.

FRONT
As back to *
Divide for neck, left side — P2 tog, P27 (29, 31), slip remaining sts on to a stitch-holder.
Working on these sts shape armhole and V-neck, all sizes:
Next row — K.
Next row — P2 tog, P to end.
Next row — K2 tog, K to end.
Next row — P2 tog, P to end.
34 in. and 36 in. sizes only —
Next row — K.
Next row — P2 tog, P to last 2 sts, P2 tog.
36 in. size only —
Next row — K.
Next row — P2 tog, P to end.
32 in. size only —
Next row — K.
Next row — P to last 2 sts, P2 tog.
36 in. size only —
Next row — K2 tog, K to end.
Next row — P.
Next row — K.
Next row — P to last 2 sts, P2 tog.
Shape V-neck —
Next row — K.
Next row — P.
Next row — K2 tog, K to end.
Next row — P.
Next row — K.
Next row — P to last 2 sts, P2 tog.
Repeat the last 6 rows four (four, three) times more.
Next row — K.
Cast off.

Right front — Rejoin yarn to hold 28 (30, 32) sts and pick up centre front st on to needle 29 (31, 33) sts.
Shape armhole and V-neck, all sizes —
Next row — P.
Next row — K2 tog, K to end.
Next row — P.
Next row — K2 tog, K to last 2 sts, K2 tog.
Next row — P.
Next row — K2 tog, K to end.
34 in. and 36 in. sizes only —
Next row — P2 tog, P to end.
Next row — K2 tog, K to end.
36 in. size only —
Next row — P.
Next row — K2 tog, K to last 2 sts, K2 tog.
32 in. size only —
Next row — P2 tog, P to end.
Next row — K.
36 in. size only —
Next row — P.
Next row — K.
Next row — P2 tog, P to end.
Next row — K.
Shape V neck —
Next row — P.
Next row — K to last 2 sts, K2 tog.
Next row — P.
Next row — K.
Next row — P2 tog, P to end.
Next row — K.
Repeat the last 6 rows four (four, three) more times.
Next row — P.
Cast off.

NECKBAND (all sizes).
With 4 mm needles and Majestic cast on 9 sts and work 200 rows garter-stitch (every row K).
Cast off.

SLEEVES (all sizes).
With 4 mm needles and Majestic cast on 45 sts and work 20 rows K1, P1 rib. Change to 6½ mm needles and Palamino and continue in stocking-stitch comm with a P row.
Work 14 rows.
Inc 1 st at beg and end of next and every following 14th row until there are 53 sts on the needle.
Continue without shaping until 70 rows Palamino have been worked from comm. Shape sleeve head — Cast off 4 sts at beg of next 2 rows (45 sts). Dec 1 st at beg of next and every following row until 17 sts remain.
Cast off.

MAKE UP
Do not press work. Join shoulder seams. Sew neckband to V-neck, overlapping right side over left at base of V. Join side and sleeve seams. Sew sleeves into armholes.

MAKING FACES!

Have you ever wanted to look this good — but simply don't know how? With our special step-by-step guide, it's suddenly all very easy! On the next four pages, we show you each stage exactly as it happens, making it simple and straightforward for you to copy. So get ready to look great — with a little help from us!

Simple Shades For Day...

Daring Colour For Nights

1. Begin working on skin that's cleansed, toned and moisturised, and draw hair back off the face. Use a cover stick to tone down any angry spots or blemishes — dot it on top of the marked areas, and blend in well with clean fingertips.

2. Apply foundation as triangular or circular wedges on the areas shown; on the centre of the forehead, down the nose, dotted on the chin, along the cheekbones and into the centre of the cheeks.

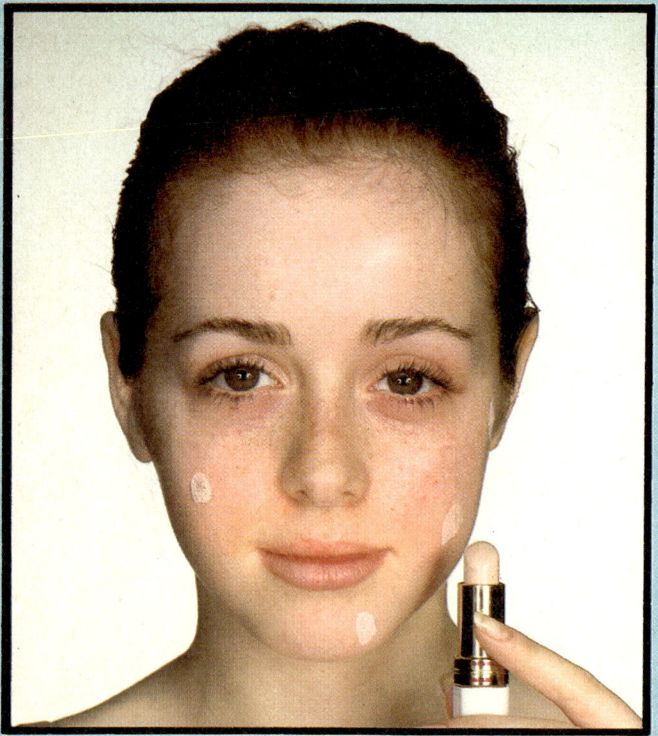

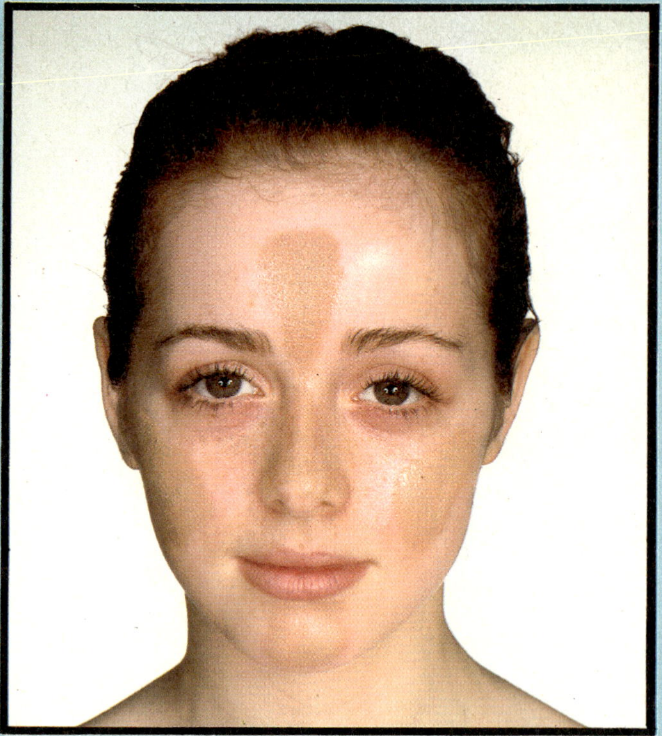

A Flawless Base

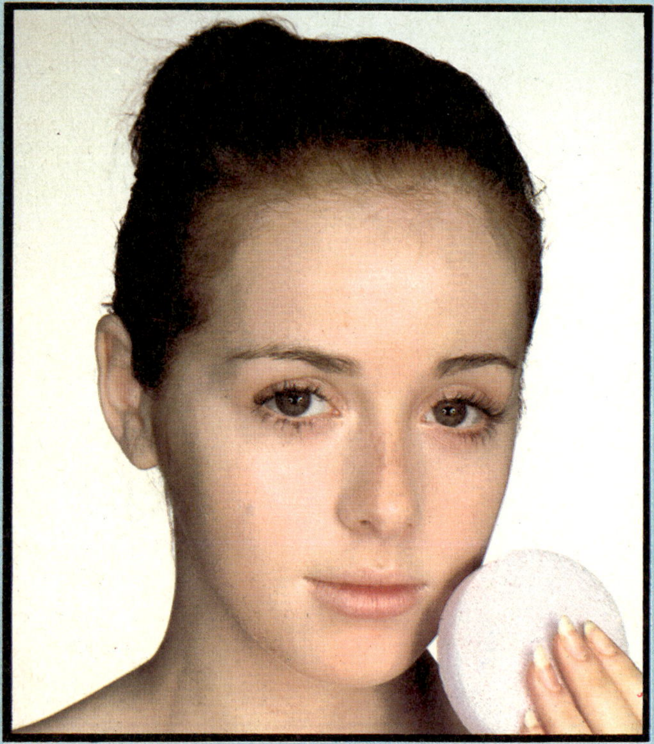

3. The best way to achieve a really even finish is to blend foundation using a damp cosmetic sponge. Blend evenly all over the face, taking special care under chin and at the hair line, making sure there is no obvious line where the colour stops.

4. To set this base, and make it last longer, finish off with loose translucent powder. Fluff on a light coating all over the face and gently dust off all excess. This is particularly helpful to oily skins.

1. For a simple day look, we chose soft gold as a basic shade, and applied it all over the eye area, on the lids taken right up to the brow bone. Eye make-up is always easier to apply and blend if you can use a good natural bristle brush — if that's not possible, use cotton wool buds. Either are better than fingertips!

2. Choose a highlighter that tones with the main eye colour — ours is a pale yellow, applied on the brow bone and blended in.

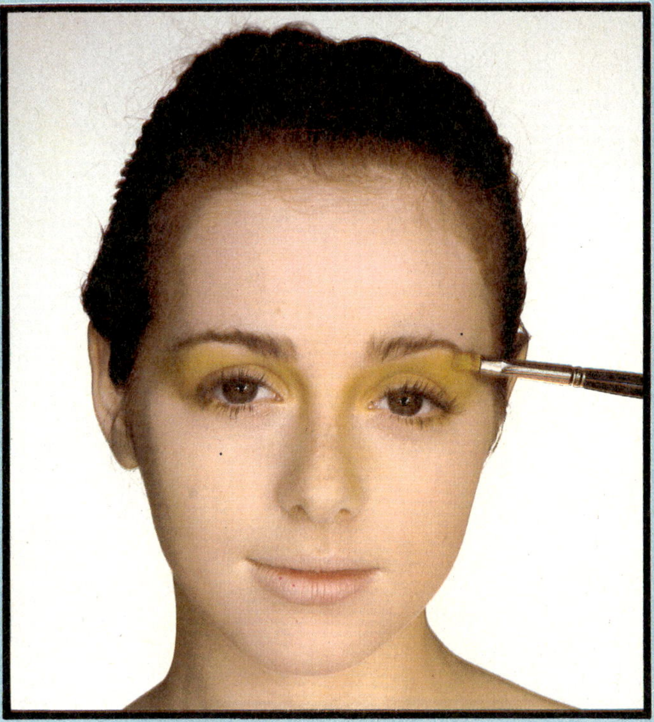

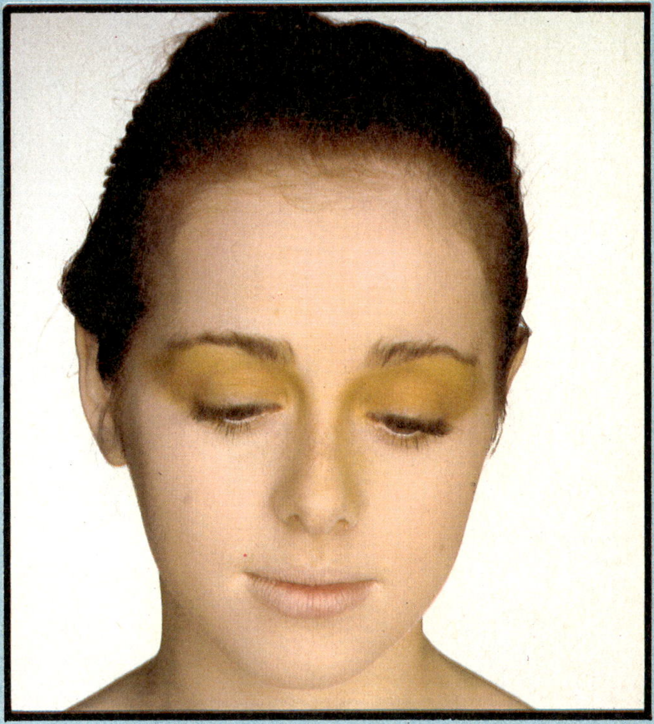

Making Eyes

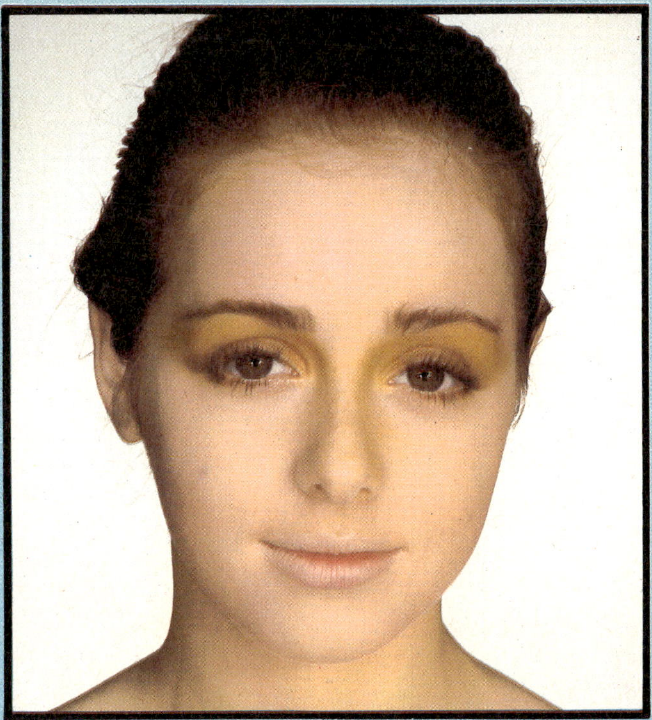

3. Use a darker shade to add definition to eyes — we chose a burnt orange applied along the socket line and on the lid, with the colour taken just under lower lashes.

4. Eye make-up never looks properly finished without mascara — you might find it easier to apply without smudging if you use a magnifying mirror. Apply two coats, on both top and bottom lashes, and don't worry about the odd smudge — they're easy to remove with the moistened tip of a cotton wool bud.

1. Apply blusher by stroking it along temples and from the centre of cheekbones to the ear lobes.

2. Blend well with a soft chunky brush, finishing with a natural look and subtle shaping.

Lips And Cheeks

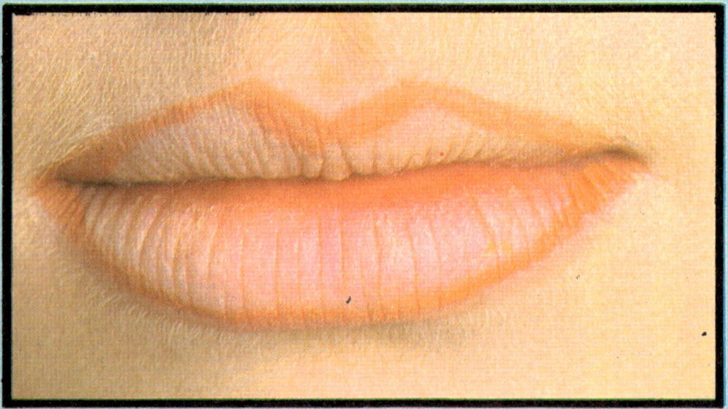

3. Outline lips with a lip pencil one shade darker than your lipstick colour, or with lipstick applied with a thin lip brush. Powder over with translucent powder to set the colour and prevent any bleeding or running of colour.

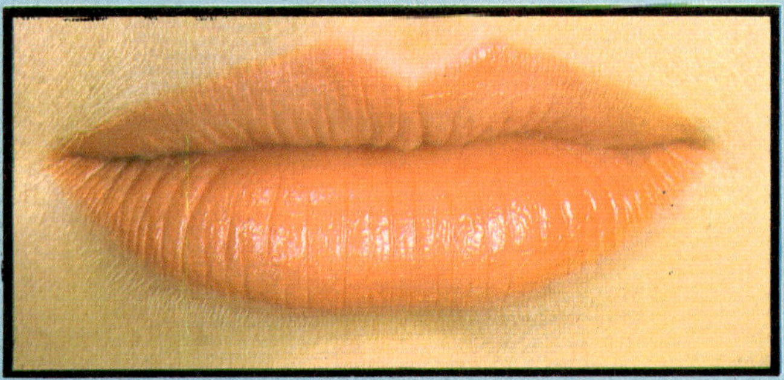

4. Fill in lips with colour, using a lip brush if you can. A tip to help colour last longer is to blot lips with a tissue and apply colour a second time.

5. The finished day look is soft and natural, but it still looks effective — it doesn't take much time, and with a little practice, you'll soon have it looking perfect.

1. Apply the basic shadow all over the eye area — we chose a soft pink shade.

2. Highlight along the brow bone — we used a pearlised pinky colour to tone.

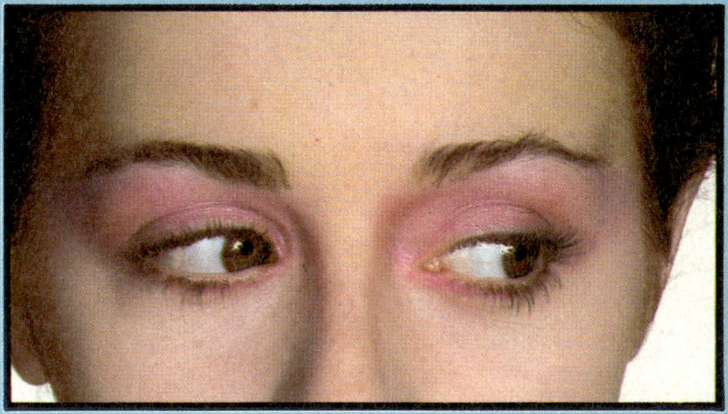

3. Eyeliner or kohl pencil add definition to eyes. Draw the colour inside lower lashes and very gently on the upper lid.

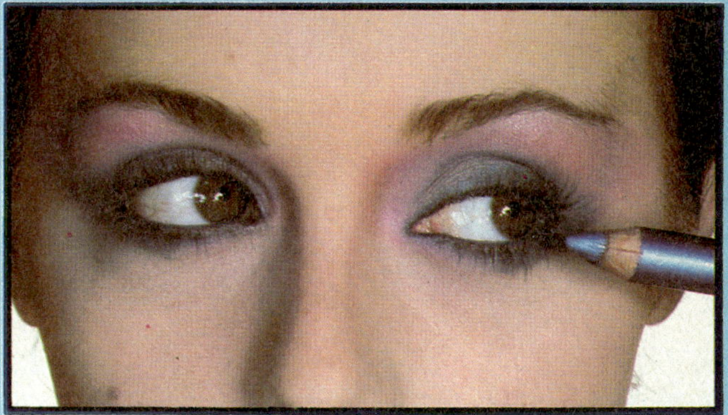

Evening Eyes

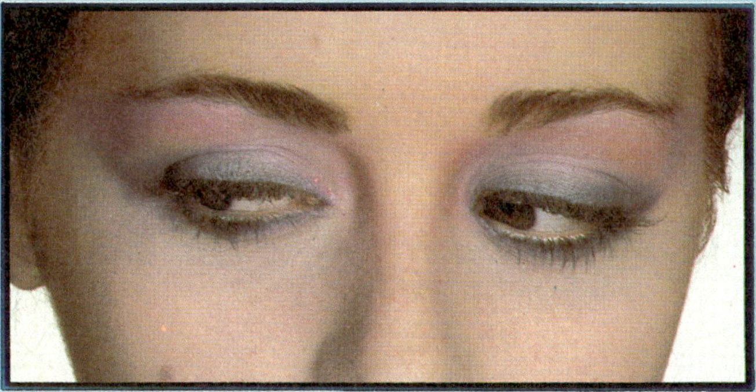

4. For a darker shade, we chose blue to contrast, applied on the eyelid with the colour taken under lower lashes.

5. Again, mascara adds the finishing touch, brushed on top and bottom lashes. For evenings, try navy or purple mascara for a touch of colour and drama.

6. The finished look for evenings is certainly eye catching — match it up with pink blusher and a bold fuchsia lip colour. It's easy when you know how, and so much fun to do!

THE OTHER DALLAS STARS...

OK, own up, all you telly addicts out there — you can bring out your stetsons from behind the sofa because it's "Dallas" time!

Don't you ever feel life is boring when you're not engrossed in the Ewing exploits?

Well, wakey, wakey, because here we have the Southfork superstars on this very page, with of course some lesser-known stars as addicted to the series as we are. We asked some of our favourite people who *their* favourite was, and here's what they told us . . . Read on and find out that everybody loves a Ewing . . .

STEVE STRANGE

Sue Ellen must have the most mobile mouth ever. It can go in twenty different directions at once! She's equal with Pam who must have the most mobile **eyes** ever — they can go in twenty different directions at once.

ROB HALFORD — Judas Priest

The best character isn't even in it now, it's Kirstin. She was so scheming and would stop at nothing to get what she wanted. She was one lady with absolutely no scruples.

THERESE BAZAR — Dollar

Miss Ellie drives me up the wall. She's so tolerant and such a martyr . . . I shudder when she gives her all-forgiving smile — and that's about fifteen times a minute!

BOB GELDOF

I don't really have much time to watch "Dallas" now because I'm usually so busy, but for sheer star appeal you can't beat Pam. She wobbles a bit, too. I wonder if you've got to have a wobble to get a part?

PHIL LYNOTT

It's got to be J.R., the evil one himself. It's wonderful that when he does something really nasty, he always manages that sly smile.

SHEENA EASTON

Oh, Sue Ellen's my favourite because it would give me great pleasure to see her get throttled. I'd really enjoy **that** episode.

IS YOUR BOY THE Town Clown?

While munching your way through an incredibly sticky toffee apple and wondering if your face looks like a luminous blob under the glare of the Big Top lights, have you ever taken time off to look really closely at all those lovely circus men and wonder what they're like in real life? In fact, *every* boy is a circus type at heart and our fun guide below tells you how to spot the similarities which are a really big giveaway to his personality. Interested? Well, read on and find out what the boy in *your* life is really like — if you dare . . .

THE BOY WHO THINKS HE'S —

THE CLOWN

WHAT HE'LL LOOK LIKE

This boy is loud in everything he does and his taste in clothes is no exception. He'll go in for bright, dazzling colours which stun at a distance of fifty paces and none of which seem to match or tone in with the rest. Perhaps he's on the lookout for laughs if things get desperate and his jokes fall flat!

HOW HE'LL ACT

He's definitely the life and soul of any party and he'll constantly amaze you with his display of wit and funny stories. He'll keep you interested by playing practical jokes on everyone in sight (which come in handy if you've got any enemies) and he'll be a big hit with your parents (as long as his jokes are clean).

HIS ADVANTAGES

He's really useful at family parties, stopping traffic and clearing long bus queues with his endless supply of corny jokes. He's also pretty good at getting on with little brothers as they've got a lot in common — they've both got to grow up yet!

HIS DISADVANTAGES

His one big failing is that he doesn't know when to shut up. He seems to think that all major disasters can be cleared up with a nod, wink and yet another Irish joke — even if you've just told him that the budgie's just snuffed it!

IF THE GOING GETS TOO ROUGH

Drop a banana skin in front of his size 10 shoes.

THE BOY WHO THINKS HE'S —

THE LION TAMER

WHAT HE'LL LOOK LIKE

Well, his safari jacket and gumboots are a big giveaway. He'll have a firm set jaw, wild, blazing eyes which could bore holes in your back at 30 paces and a very definite frown which is usually reserved for people (or lions) who in his opinion are misbehaving!

HOW HE'LL ACT

This guy's behaviour will certainly be anything but normal. In fact, even walking down the street with him will show you that he's not the type to stand any nonsense. Everyday things such as little boys on roller skates knocking down old ladies as they go, are situations worthy of his attention, and before you know it the unsuspecting child will be skating on the left hand side of the pavement and giving way to oncoming prams and shopping trolleys!

HIS ADVANTAGES

He's certainly very useful to have around when threatened by wild beasts (your little brother in a temper), or if you're being jostled in the bus queue. One glance is usually all that's needed to let them know who's boss and woe betide anyone who needs a second glance — gulp . . .

HIS DISADVANTAGES

His confidence can be a bit off-putting at times, especially as he thinks he knows it all when it comes to handling girls! He'll try to organise your life, control your behaviour and even decide on what you'll wear — just to let everyone know who's boss.

IF THE GOING GETS TOO ROUGH

Stick your paws in the air and pretend you're dead!

THE BOY WHO THINKS HE'S —

THE JUGGLER

WHAT HE'LL LOOK LIKE

Well, it's fair to say that this guy is all hands, and if you ever get close enough to hold one you'll see what we mean!

HOW HE'LL ACT

He'll amaze you with his ability to cope with several situations all at the one time — and handle them successfully!

HIS ADVANTAGES

He's great to have around when organising parties or any other kind of get-togethers as he'll keep things moving along without batting an eyelid (even if the disco hasn't turned up yet and the crisps are soggy — don't worry, he'll cope).

HIS DISADVANTAGES

As he obviously likes to have a lot of things going for him at the one time, it's not two-timing you'll have to worry about, but possibly three, four, or even five-timing! He's likely to try to fit you into his tight schedule at short notice, so unless you fancy dashing off to meet him with your hair still wet and wearing a bath towel — forget it.

IF THE GOING GETS TOO ROUGH

Slip through his fingers!

Well, now that you know how to spot the difference between all those circus types, it shouldn't be too hard to bring their act to an end if you don't fancy an encore. But on the other hand, if you do, with all this new-found knowledge you'll have them jumping through hoops and doing exactly what you want!

IT'LL BE BETTER THIS TIME...

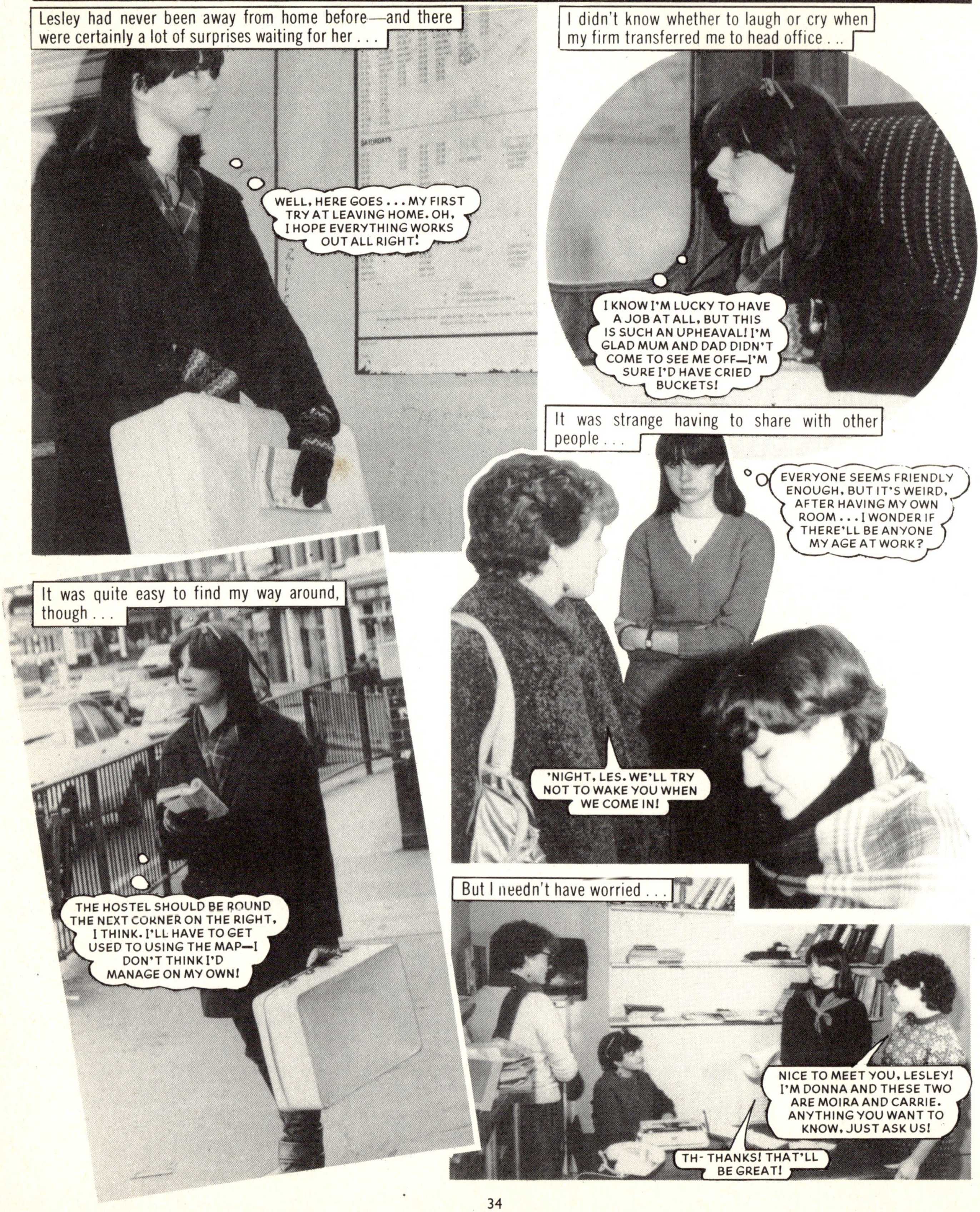

It was a bit depressing, having to go back to the hostel, though . . .
EVERYONE SEEMS TO BE GOING OUT. I SUPPOSE I'LL JUST HAVE TO READ, OR SOMETHING! THIS PLACE IS OK, BUT I'D LOVE SOMEWHERE OF MY OWN— OR EVEN SHARING . . .
And over the next month, I went home every weekend . . .
OH LESLEY, IT'S SO NICE TO SEE YOU! TAKE YOUR COAT OFF AND TELL ME WHAT YOU'VE BEEN DOING!
IT'S GREAT TO SEE YOU TOO, MUM! WHAT'S FOR TEA? I'M STARVING!
Then, one day at work . . .
THE HOSTEL'S BEGINNING TO GET ME DOWN A BIT. THERE'S NO PRIVACY AT ALL.
I DIDN'T REALISE YOU WERE STILL THERE! LISTEN, I'VE GOT AN IDEA. I'M STILL LIVING AT HOME, BUT . . .
Donna suggested we share a flat—and I jumped at the chance . . .
WELL, WE SHOULD COME UP WITH SOMETHING FROM THIS LOT!
I CAN'T WAIT TO START LOOKING. IT'LL BE FANTASTIC, HAVING A PLACE OF OUR OWN!
It took ages to find somewhere, but . . .
I THINK THIS COULD LOOK REALLY GOOD WITH A BIT OF REORGANISING! WHAT ABOUT YOU, LES?
SUITS ME! I'D EVEN ENJOY THE DECORATING!
And so I phoned Mum to tell her . . .
IT'S GREAT MUM! IT'LL NEED TIDYING UP, OF COURSE, BUT THERE ARE TWO OF US AND DONNA'S A GREAT LAUGH! WE GET ON REALLY WELL.
AS LONG AS YOU'RE SURE, DEAR! AND LET US KNOW IF YOU NEED ANYTHING!

We had to wait a few weeks, but finally . . .
WHEW! I DIDN'T KNOW I HAD SO MUCH JUNK!
ME NEITHER. COME ON—LET'S GET THIS LOT SORTED OUT AND WE CAN HAVE A CUP OF COFFEE. I'LL NEED IT!
It took ages . . .
WELL, I'M NOT DOING ANY MORE TODAY. THIS ROOM'LL HAVE TO WAIT. WE'D BETTER GET SOME FOOD IN, THOUGH.
YOU GO, THEN, AND I'LL CARRY ON.
But when I got back . . .
HEY—I THOUGHT YOU WERE GOING TO UNPACK!
THERE'S NO RUSH—NOBODY TO ORDER US AROUND NOW, IS THERE?
OH, BY THE WAY, MAGGIE FROM THE OFFICE IS HAVING A PARTY TONIGHT—FANCY GOING ALONG?
BUT WE CAN'T JUST LEAVE ALL THIS!
OF COURSE WE CAN! IT WON'T TAKE LONG TOMORROW AND YOU'VE NOT BEEN TO A PARTY HERE YET, HAVE YOU?
WELL, I SUPPOSE NOT. AND I DO QUITE FANCY A PARTY . . .
And in the end . . .
LIKE TO DANCE, LESLEY?
THANKS, I'D LOVE TO!
I'M REALLY GLAD I CAME, NOW. THIS IS BETTER THAN SHIFTING FURNITURE, ANY DAY!
And for a while, everything was great . . .
WHAT ON EARTH HAVE YOU GOT THERE?
A TELLY, YOU IDIOT—WHAT DOES IT LOOK LIKE? I'LL BE PAYING FOR IT FOR MONTHS, BUT IT'LL BE WORTH IT!
Life was certainly never dull . . .
COME ON LES—THAT LOT WILL LYNCH ME IF THEY DON'T GET THEIR COFFEE SOON!
OK, OK—I'M COMING.

HERE WE ARE—ANNETTE, YOURS IS WITHOUT MILK, ISN'T IT?
THAT'S RIGHT. THANKS LES.
WE WERE JUST SAYING HOW TERRIFIC THE FLAT LOOKS. WISH WE HAD SOMEPLACE LIKE THIS.
But sometimes, Donna was really irritating . . .
GIVE ME A HAND WITH THE DISHES, WILL YOU DONNA? I DID ALL THE COOKING.
OH, LET'S LEAVE IT FOR NOW. WE CAN DO IT IN THE MORNING!
And after that, it got worse . . .
DONNA, PLEASE TURN THE STEREO DOWN. I'M REALLY TIRED—I JUST CAN'T GET TO SLEEP!
OK, KEEP YOUR HAIR ON! IT'S NOT THAT LOUD!
And . . .
OH NO! DONNA PROMISED SHE'D CLEAN UP THIS MESS BEFORE SHE WENT OUT. IT'LL TAKE ME AGES!
AND THERE'S NOTHING HERE FOR TONIGHT'S MEAL! WHAT ON EARTH'S SHE PLAYING AT?
And when she finally got in . . .
DONNA, I'D LIKE A WORD—
OH, LES, YOU SHOULD'VE COME TO THE DISCO TONIGHT! YOU REALLY MISSED YOURSELF. I MET A REALLY SPECIAL BOY—HIS NAME'S DREW!
I didn't want to spoil things, but when Drew came round . . .
H- HELLO! I DIDN'T REALISE YOU WERE HERE!
HI—I'M DREW. DONNA'S TOLD ME ABOUT YOU!

He was awful, but Donna just adored him . . .
THEY NEVER EVEN ASKED ME IF I MINDED HAVING A PARTY OR NOT! AND DREW'S FRIENDS ARE JUST AS BAD AS HE IS! WE'LL HAVE THE POLICE HERE IN A MINUTE IF THEY DON'T WATCH OUT!
I tried to talk to Donna next day, but . . .
DON'T BE SO WET! THERE'S NO REAL DAMAGE, EXCEPT FOR A COUPLE OF BROKEN GLASSES. WE CAN SOON CLEAR IT UP!
I CAN, YOU MEAN! LOOK DONNA, I'M FED UP RUNNING AFTER YOU— THIS TIME YOU CAN JUST DO IT YOURSELF.
But when I got back after a weekend at home . . .
HI, DREW! WHAT ARE YOU DOING HERE?
JUST MAKING MYSELF AT HOME. I'M STAYING!
I was really mad . . .
AND JUST WHY DOES DREW HAVE TO STAY HERE?
HE'S BEEN CHUCKED OUT OF HIS FLAT AND HE'S GOT NOWHERE ELSE TO GO! IT'S ONLY FOR A LITTLE WHILE, LES— BE REASONABLE!
But I couldn't help worrying . . .
I DON'T TRUST DREW— THERE'S SOMETHING REALLY SHIFTY ABOUT HIM! AND DONNA'S CHANGED SO MUCH SINCE SHE MET HIM . . .
And he was still there after a fortnight!
HURRY UP WITH THE GRUB, LES! I'M STARVING.
I THOUGHT YOU WERE SUPPOSED TO BE MOVING OUT TODAY?
YOU MIND YOUR OWN BUSINESS! DONNA DOESN'T MIND ME STAYING AND IT'S GOT NOTHING TO DO WITH YOU, ANYWAY!
WELL, YOU NEEDN'T THINK I'M COOKING ANY MORE MEALS FOR YOU! GET IT YOURSELF!
And next morning things really came to a head . . .
OOPS, 'SCUSE ME! PHONE FOR YOU, LES— SOUNDS LIKE YOUR OLD MAN!
WHAT? OH NO!

WHO WAS THAT BOY, LESLEY? WHAT'S HE DOING THERE AT THIS TIME IN THE MORNING?
HE'S—HE'S A FRIEND OF DONNA'S, DAD—
But I knew he didn't believe me . . .
NOW HE WANTS ME HOME STRAIGHT AWAY! HOW ON EARTH CAN I GET DAD TO UNDERSTAND? I DON'T EVEN LIKE DREW!
I had to go home anyway, though, so . . .
MY GRAN'S HAD A HEART ATTACK AND I'VE GOT TO GO HOME FOR A BIT, DONNA. DAD WAS FURIOUS ABOUT DREW! HE THINKS—WELL, YOU CAN IMAGINE WHAT HE THINKS!
LOOK, DONNA—WHILE I'M AWAY, TRY TO FIND DREW SOMEWHERE ELSE TO STAY—PLEASE. OTHERWISE I WON'T BE ALLOWED BACK HERE TO LIVE.
WELL, I'M NOT GOING TO THROW HIM OUT! JUST EXPLAIN—IT'LL BE ALL RIGHT!
But at home . . .
I BELIEVE WHAT YOU'RE TELLING ME, LESLEY, BUT I'M NOT HAPPY ABOUT IT. I THINK YOU SHOULD COME HOME!
BUT WHAT ABOUT MY JOB? I JUST CAN'T LEAVE!
YOU'LL FIND SOMETHING LOCALLY, LOVE. THE WHOLE THING JUST SEEMS SO UNSATIS-FACTORY!
I KNOW, BUT I'LL NEVER FIND A JOB—I WAS TRANSFERRED BECAUSE THERE WAS NO WORK FOR ME HERE!
And by the time I left . . .
YOU'VE GOT TO GET THINGS SORTED OUT, LESLEY!
WE'LL WAIT UNTIL THE WEEK, LOVE, BUT AFTER THAT, YOU'RE COMING HOME. THAT GIRL'S A BAD INFLUENCE!
I'LL HAVE TO DO SOMETHING, BUT WHAT?

And when I got back . . .
WHAT ON EARTH—? DONNA, WHAT'S HAPPENED?
OH, LESLEY, IT'S TERRIBLE!
YOU'LL NEVER FORGIVE ME—I'VE BEEN SUCH A FOOL! AND NOW I DON'T KNOW WHAT TO DO!
IT WAS YESTERDAY—I WENT OUT SHOPPING IN THE AFTERNOON AND WHEN I GOT BACK, EVERYTHING HAD GONE!
BUT WASN'T DREW HERE?
DON'T YOU UNDERSTAND? HE TOOK IT ALL, AND I HAVEN'T EVEN FINISHED PAYING FOR THE TELEVISION YET! I'LL PROBABLY END UP IN COURT OR SOMETHING!
I didn't know what to say . . .
IT'LL BE OK, DONNA! WE'LL WORK SOMETHING OUT.
WHAT? I HAVEN'T EVEN GOT ENOUGH TO PAY THE RENT! HE TOOK ALL MY SAVINGS—AND I THOUGHT HE LOVED ME!
And then . . .
LOOK, DONNA, I'M GOING TO RING MY PARENTS. THEY'LL HELP US UNTIL EVERYTHING'S SORTED OUT. THEN WE'LL HAVE TO TELL THE POLICE—THAT WAY WE MIGHT GET SOME OF THE STUFF BACK!
. . . SO WE CAN BOTH COME HOME FOR A FEW DAYS? DONNA'S IN A TERRIBLE STATE!
OF COURSE, LOVE. WHAT A DREADFUL THING TO HAPPEN!

Once we'd spoken to the police and our boss, we went home . . .
OH LESLEY, YOUR PARENTS MUST REALLY THINK THE WORST OF ME! AND I CAN'T BLAME THEM!
STOP WORRYING—THEY WON'T EAT YOU!
And . . .
COME IN, YOU TWO! YOU LOOK TIRED OUT!
OH THANKS, MUM! IT'S SUCH A RELIEF TO BE HOME.
We had a meal and Donna explained . . .
I KNOW IT WAS STUPID OF ME TO TRUST HIM, MR BROOKS, BUT—WELL, HE SEEMED TO TAKE A REAL INTEREST IN ME, AND NOBODY'S DONE THAT FOR A LONG WHILE . . .
YOU'VE HAD A BAD TIME, DONNA—WE KNOW THAT . . .
IT'S A HORRIBLE THING TO HAVE TO GO THROUGH!
MUM AND DAD SEEM QUITE SYMPATHETIC. I'M SURE THEY'LL UNDERSTAND . . .
And . . .
WELL, IF YOU AGREE, DONNA, WE CAN LEND YOU THE MONEY TO KEEP BOTH OF YOU GOING UNTIL EVERYTHING'S SORTED OUT. WOULD THAT HELP?
OH, IT'D BE WONDERFUL! BUT SURELY—
YOU SEE? I TOLD YOU EVERYTHING WOULD WORK OUT FINE!
I CAN'T BELIEVE IT! I NEVER THOUGHT YOUR PARENTS WOULD BE SO NICE—ESPECIALLY WHEN I WAS SO AWFUL!
WELL, FROM NOW ON, YOU DO YOUR SHARE OF THE CLEANING! OK?
I'LL EVEN POLISH THE LIGHTBULBS!
DON'T GET CARRIED AWAY, DONNA! I MIGHT HOLD YOU TO THAT!
I DON'T MIND! THIS TIME, WE'RE REALLY GOING TO MAKE A GO OF THINGS—I JUST KNOW IT!
THE END

Who's A Pretty Boy

Long, long ago, the last thing on a boy's mind was how to attract a girl. He just dotted her one on the head with his trusty club and hauled her off to his cave.

Today, though, life's a lot more complicated, and relationships are a lot more subtle. The me-Tarzan-you-Jane approach doesn't work now that there are more fellas around than girls (what a nice arrangement!) and boys are thinking more and more about the image they project.

We spoke to some boys and asked them how they saw themselves in the attractiveness stakes and jokingly asked how they'd rate themselves on a scale of 1-10. Here's what we came up with . . .

Steven, who's eighteen, works in a bank.

"I'm pretty average really; average height and build so I'd guess I'd rate a five. I'm just not the sort of bloke who could pull birds by sheer looks alone. If you put me in a shop window, there'd be no queues!

"I've had a couple of nice girlfriends, who were really special, and luckily they got to know the real me first – I can't say it was my looks really. My present girlfriend thinks I'm fantastic, so who am I to argue?

"I'm still living at home, which is a bit restrictive. I suppose I dream of branching out, getting a flat and changing my image completely. I'd love to be someone like Sting. I can't help feeling that I'm missing out on some things. Maybe I should be more outrageous and daring in my life – but even if the chances came along I don't know how I'd react."

Steven sounds like a pretty honest, reliable guy, a boy to trust — but is that the type the girls really go for? Here's Paul, and he's just the opposite. He's good looking *and* he knows it.

"Ten I'd rate – sure, why not! I have no bother attracting girls. I suppose I look the part. I'm pleased with the way I look. Life must be a lot less interesting if you're ugly. Knowing girls fancy you gives you confidence.

"I'm never short of dates but if it's too easy I lose interest and cool off. I enjoy the chatting-up bit. Mind you, I never crawl. But if a girl plays a little bit hard to get, she's got me interested.

"Sometimes I do get the feeling I'm putting on an act all the time, trying to impress. I hear myself trotting out the same old lines with a new girl. Sometimes I don't like myself much and I get fed up playing the scene, but I couldn't see myself sticking to one girl. What a waste!"

Paul certainly knows what he wants, and a lot of girls find that attractive. Bob, on the other hand, hasn't got any confidence at all. He's still at school.

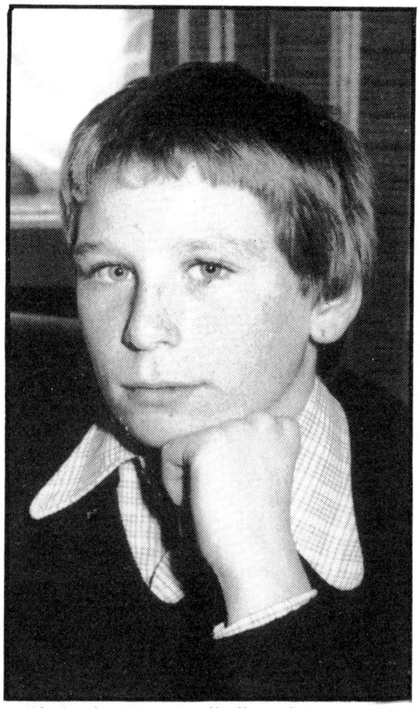

"I don't rate at all. I'm sixteen and I look about thirteen, and I don't know one girl who isn't put off by that. They all go for the big guys, the guys who look older than they do, so that means I'd have to get someone at primary school!

"I think girls go for looks first and foremost. I mean at a disco, if you ask a girl to dance she gives you the once over and if you don't match up she'll turn you down. It's pretty unfair.

"Maybe I'm not meeting the right girls but the ones I meet, especially at school, are pretty hard. Although everyone says it's personality that counts, they want a fella with looks and a bit of cash to spend on them – and I don't have either."

Are we really that bad? Tony is a guy who has the looks but he hasn't got a girlfriend at the moment. He's an assistant in a photographic shop.

"I'd rate five on a good day! I've never gone out with a girl for longer than two months and it's been ages since I asked a girl out because I get more and more scared of being

turned down. It gets worse as you get older, I think. You tend to take things more seriously.

"It's rotten being a bloke, having to be pushy, having to chat up a girl when you're just not sure whether she's interested or not.

"There have been a couple of times I've met a girl and well, kind of backed off at the last minute. Afterwards, I go over what she's said in my head and half the time I realise that it was all my fault. I should have been more positive – asked to see her home, asked her out, at least asked for her phone number, but I always lose my nerve **and** *the girl.*

"It's just a basic lack of confidence in myself. It even extends to my work – if I was more pushy I'd get a great job as a photographer on a paper maybe, instead of wasting my time here."

Are girls so frightening, then? Are they only after guys with looks? Next, we asked a few of the monsters themselves — the girls — for their opinions of boys, and they weren't shy to tell us what they thought!

Julie is a girl who has strong feelings, and surprisingly, the boys she doesn't like are the nice ones . . .

"Nice guys are boring. I don't even like handsome types – I like interesting types. Somehow I'm always more attracted to boys who treat me badly – who don't phone when they say they

Then?

will, who stand me up, or two-time me. It's much more exciting!

"Sure, I shed a lot of tears but I'd hate to be stuck in the safe 'two nights a week and every weekend' routine some of my friends are in."

That's quite a surprising attitude and one probably not many girls share, but it takes all kinds. Karen is good looking and she freely admits to judging a bloke by his looks.

"I'm lucky because I can pick and choose the type of guy I want. I go weak at the knees for skinny blokes who've got good dress sense. If a guy doesn't make the effort with how he looks then I'm not interested.

"I know I couldn't go out with someone who wasn't good looking, because every time we went out I'd feel embarrassed with him and I'd be wishing I was with someone else."

So what about the ideal imaginary muscle man? The truth is, he just doesn't exist. So next time you feel you've got no chance with a boy just stop and think that he's probably feeling as terrified as *you*!

The thing to remember is that when you're looking through the eyes of love, *everybody's* gorgeous!

GETTING FRUITY! Something For (Almost) Nothing

Make yourself a bag that's roomy enough to hold schoolbooks, shopping and all your junk — it couldn't be easier! All you need to make the kind of bag shown here is a piece of denim or canvas, any old leftover paint lying around the house and one or two fruits or vegetables.

The sort of material you use to make the bag is really up to you, but it should be strong and fairly light in colour. Off-white denim or canvas is ideal and a piece 50 cms. by 115 cms., which is the amount you need, shouldn't cost much more than £1.

Once you've got hold of the material, the first thing you have to do to make your bag is to print a design on it. Take one of the fruits or vegetables which you've chosen — an apple, for instance — and cut it in half.

Now lay your piece of material out flat on a table, or on the floor. Using a small brush, coat the cut side of your fruit with a thin coat of paint and then print this on to your fabric.

Repeat this procedure all over the material, printing either at random or building up a pattern. You can, of course, use different fruits and print them in various colours. For instance, we used an apple printed in orange, red and black.

You can use any type of household paint to decorate your bag although the easiest to apply is non-drip emulsion — don't try to use water colours as these will wash out.

Most fruits and vegetables will print well as long as they aren't *too* juicy. You can't, for instance, print a plum very easily as it'll squash. If you decide to use an onion, leave it in a warm place for a few hours after cutting it in half, because this will make the rings stand out more and give a better print.

Once you've printed your material, hang it up and leave it to dry for about 12 hours.

When the pattern is dry, cut two strips, each about 8 cms. wide, from one of the shorter edges of the material — these are to make the handles. Take one of these strips and fold it in half lengthways with the pattern inside. Now sew the strip along one short edge and one long edge to make a tube. Using a knitting needle, blunt end first, push the closed edge down the tube, thus turning the handle the right way out and revealing the pattern. Do this with both handles.

Next, take the large piece of material and fold in a strip about 1 cm. wide along each short edge. Stitch these and then attach the handles to them by sewing their

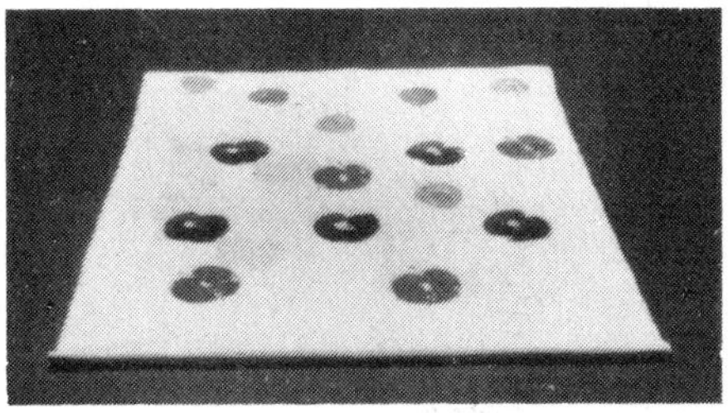

The material with the fruit prints on it.

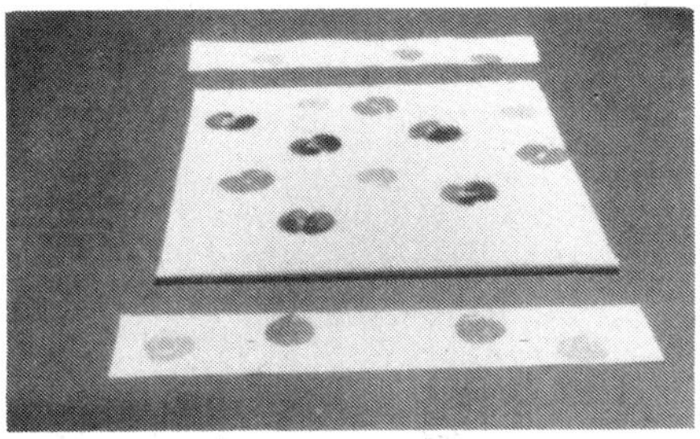

Cut two strips off the material. These are used to make the handles.

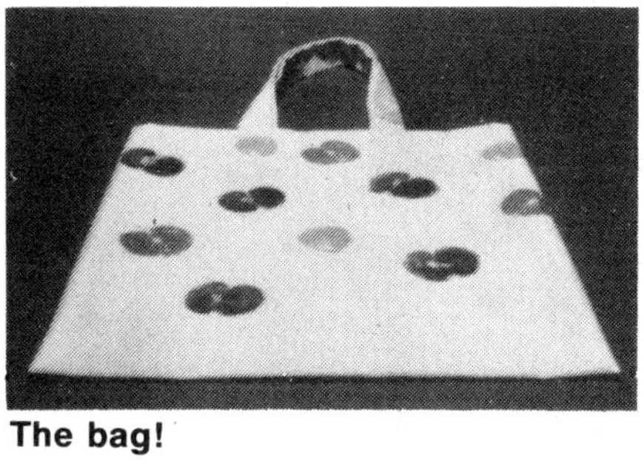

The bag!

ends to these hems, leaving a gap of about 20 cms. between each end.

You should now have a large, flat piece of material with a handle at each end. Now fold this in half, with the pattern on the inside, and sew along the edges, leaving you with an inside out bag. Finally, iron the seams open and turn the bag inside out to reveal the pattern.

With a little care, and about two hours work, you'll have made yourself a shopping bag, one that's pretty unique and totally different from anything you could buy in the shops!

I Only Wanted

EVEN now, I can still remember the horrible, sinking sensation in the pit of my stomach as I sat in the kitchen, facing my parents, saying over and over again to myself that it wasn't true.

"Look, love, I know it's hard — it's hard for all of us, but the factory *is* closing down," Dad'd said bluntly.

"So, along with all the rest of the men, I've been given a choice. Either I accept redundancy pay, or I can be transferred to Newcastle to the same kind of job."

"But — but Newcastle's miles away," I wailed.

I suppose I should have felt guilty as I saw Dad run a despairing hand through his hair and quietly explain that there were no jobs to be found around here and that the Newcastle offer was his only hope, but I didn't.

"Well I'm not going," I said tearfully. "All my friends are here. I'm just not going . . ."

"None of us want to leave our friends," Mum soothed, "but sometimes things like this happen and, well, things have to change."

"Not for me, they don't," I snapped.

For the rest of the evening I stayed in my room, too miserable to move, and with the same question running through my mind. How was I going to tell Greg?

We'd been going out together for six whole blissful months and I was really keen on him. I couldn't bear the thought of losing him, but Mum and Dad didn't seem to have any sympathy.

"Don't be silly, Ellen," Mum said wearily. "You're only fifteen. You'll have plenty more boyfriends.

"Why, I'll bet that in six months time you won't even remember who Greg is!"

But I knew that wasn't true.

I was practically in tears the next day when I finally told him the awful news, but much to my amazement he took it really well.

"HEY, don't look so glum," he smiled, "there's always the school holidays — it's not the end of the world, you know!"

The thought that I would see him again at the summer break was the only thing that kept me going during those next few miserable weeks when I had to leave school, and say goodbye to the friends I'd known all my life.

But it didn't take me long after we'd moved to realise that Greg hadn't meant the things he'd said after all.

He did write, but his letters were neither frequent nor romantic and, after about two months, they stopped altogether.

Perhaps things wouldn't have been so bad if I'd been able to settle down happily to my new life. But I couldn't. Everything about it was just so different.

Mum and Dad had been desperate for accommodation and they'd had to take the first thing they were offered, so we ended up in a poky, two-bedroomed flat in a high-rise block.

My new school was a horrible old Victorian building right in the town centre.

But worst of all was the fact that I couldn't seem to make any new friends. All the girls in my form had their own friends, and they didn't seem to have room for an outsider like me.

And all the best looking boys had steady girlfriends, so it didn't look as if there would be a new romance in my life either.

BUT then one day, when I'd been at my new school for about three months, I met Danny and, suddenly, everything changed.

Danny was tall and good looking with short dark hair and an earring, which was something that always seemed to make me go weak at the knees!

I knew Mum and Dad would have a fit if they saw me with a boy like him, but I didn't care about that.

I'd met Danny and his friends one night after school. They were sitting on the wall outside and as I passed, Karen, Danny's little sister, called out to me.

"That's a nice watch you've got," she said.

I stopped, surprised that anyone had actually bothered to speak to me! Usually I spent most of my time on my own.

"Mum and Dad gave it to me last Christmas," I replied cheerfully.

"I wouldn't mind having a watch like that," Karen smiled, "in fact, I think I'll get myself one when I'm in town tomorrow!"

For some reason everyone started to laugh at that point and I joined in as it seemed the right thing to do.

"Hey, why don't you come with us, Ellen?" Danny smiled.

"That — that would be nice," I managed. How could I refuse — every time he looked in my direction I just melted.

So, without giving it another thought, I said yes.

I had a great time on Saturday. I'd nipped into the chemists while Karen went with Danny and Lee to get the watch, and it really did look very expensive as she proudly showed it off to the rest of the gang.

"That must have cost a small fortune!" I whistled.

"Yeah," Danny laughed, "to most people but that's nothing to our Karen, is it?"

The others started to laugh too and somehow I found myself joining in.

I didn't know what Danny had meant but I didn't want to ask him. He only got angry when I asked him questions — any sort of questions.

That Saturday was the start of many happy days I spent with Danny. He was such good fun to be with and at last I felt I was beginning to settle down.

The only annoying thing was that my new friends weren't in the same class as I was at school. They were all in a lower stream.

Still, I decided I could easily remedy that by falling behind with my work. Then I'd be put down to join them.

Mum and Dad didn't seem to mind me going out so often. They knew that I'd made some new friends and said that as long as I was happy so were they.

So my new life began to take shape. I did as little work as was possible at school and I spent the evenings and weekends with Danny and his mates.

THEN, one night, my happiness turned into a horrible nightmare. We all met at the usual time, but instead of going down to the café Danny suggested that we all went over to Muirfield.

It was an estate of detached houses and I was curious as to why Danny wanted us to go there, but I didn't say anything.

When we got there, though, I wished a thousand times that I had!

It was dark by the time we reached Lowden Road and suddenly Danny's voice cut through the general chatter.

"Right, is everyone ready?" he hissed. "And for goodness sake don't hang around afterwards!"

I stood, too afraid to move, as I watched Danny and the rest of them start to pull the phone box on the corner apart! Then they started to spray the adjoining wall with paint from an aerosol and pull up flowers from the garden!

I was terrified as I watched Danny, who'd obviously organised the whole thing and I tried to hold back the tears. It was then that it suddenly dawned on me where all the money and expensive things they had came from — they were thieves as well as vandals!

I was still standing there when a van drew up on the other side of the road. The noise of the door slamming disturbed them and at Danny's command they ran in various directions.

Then, I felt a vice-like grip on the back of my shoulder and turned round to see a burly policeman standing behind me.

"I know you weren't the only one," he replied gruffly as I started to garble on about how I didn't know what he was talking about.

A few minutes later, Danny and all the others were bundled into the van by two other policeman so it was no good pretending.

"I thought you were following me, Ellen," Danny said casually, as we drove off. But I knew that wasn't true.

Danny couldn't have cared less about what happened to me. When it came to the crunch, all he and the others cared about was saving their own skins.

To Belong

SITTING in that police van, I suddenly realised what had been wrong all along. *I* was the newcomer, so I should have made the first move, but I'd waited for others to come forward when I started going around with Danny and his mates, and of course, nobody had.

Mum and Dad looked really hurt when they came to collect me from the police station and when we got home I completely broke down and tried to explain why it had all happened. I suppose I'd tried to replace Greg with Danny and I'd ignored the fact that he was a trouble-maker because I was so afraid of being alone again.

But now that's what I am — alone. Everyone at school knows that I was involved and now people not only ignore me, but avoid me as well.

Our case comes up before the Children's Panel next week and I'll probably be placed on probation which is something that'll go against me all my life.

We're supposed to learn by our mistakes, but in this case, the price of experience was a high one — a very high one indeed . . .

You'll Meet The

WHEN Sue arrived at work that morning the first thing she noticed was Linda's smile. It wasn't there. Linda was just about the most cheerful girl in the office. Rain or shine, snow, sleet or hail, nothing ever stopped Linda turning up looking happy.

Until today.

She went over and sat on her desk. "What's the matter, Linda?" she asked.

"Oh, nothing," Linda said airily, "nothing at all."

"Come on," Sue wheedled. "You can tell me. A trouble halved is a trouble shared, and all that rubbish."

Linda sighed. "What I don't need right now," she said, "is a friend quoting wise old sayings to me and getting them wrong. It's — A trouble shared is a trouble halved."

"Well, I was close," Sue said.

Linda sighed again. "If you must know, I've finished with Martin. Or Martin's finished with me. Take your pick. Either way, it's all over between us."

"Oh," Sue said. "What a shame."

"That's one way of putting it."

Sue tried again. "I mean . . . I am sorry, Linda. I know how you feel.

"No, I don't know how you feel, but if Martin was *my* boy and he'd given *me* up I'd know how you feel."

Then Mrs Barden, the office supervisor, came in and demanded to know why Sue was sitting on a desk when she should be working.

At her own desk, half-heartedly typing invoices, Sue thought about Linda and felt sorry for her. They'd looked so right for each other, Linda and Martin.

Linda's blonde beauty sort of set off Martin's dark good looks perfectly.

She must be broken hearted, Sue thought. *I know I would be. I'd be devastated. I'd carry his memory for the rest of my life and never look at another boy.*

Then she thought, *Just a minute. It's Linda he's given up, not you. He's only seen you about three times and then he probably didn't even notice you.*

She looked up to see Mrs Barden standing over her, waving a handful of typed invoices.

"Miss Wright," Mrs Barden said, "these invoices are for Messrs. Markwick & Lowe.

"You have addressed every one to Messrs. Martin with Love."

"Oh," Sue said. "Sorry."

SHE didn't get another chance to talk to Linda until lunchtime in the canteen. Linda sat toying with a plate of salad while Sue indulged in her usual sausages and chips and jelly and ice-cream.

"I suppose I'll get over it in time," Linda said. "There are plenty of other boys."

"Not like Martin," Sue said.

Linda looked at her. "Susan, I'm trying to look on the bright side. I don't need you to make me feel worse."

"There are plenty of other boys," Sue said. "You're right."

"Not like Martin," Linda said miserably. She pushed her plate aside. "I can't eat."

Sue put down her knife and fork. "Neither can I."

"I'm the one who's upset and depressed," Linda said. "There's no reason for you to stop eating."

"Oh, all right," Sue said, and picked up her knife and fork again.

"You can go off your food when some guy you fancy gives you the push," Linda said.

"I never get near enough to a guy I fanc to get the push," Sue said.

"I think it's my ears. The way they stic out."

"You've got lovely ears," Linda said.

"They stick out," Sue complained. "An if it's not my ears then it's my mouth. To wide. Or my nose.

"Have you ever looked closely at my nose?"

Linda looked at Sue's nose. "It's a perfectl good nose, Sue."

"Oh, yes, perfectly good for breathin through. Otherwise, it's ridiculous."

Linda shook her head. "You've got a lovel face, Sue," she said. "Where do you get th idea from that you're ugly?"

Sue pointed her fork at Linda.

"Aha!" she said. "I didn't say I was ugly so I must be or you wouldn't have mentione it."

Linda smiled. The first real smile of the day.

"Oh, Sue," she said. "You're a lovely girl Look at your figure. It's perfect.

"You can eat anything you lik and you don't put on weight."

"I'm skinny," Sue said.

"There you go again. Your problem is that you don't have any confidence in yourself."

"Neither would you, if you were me," Sue said.

Linda sighed heavily. "Look, I'm the one who's supposed to be feeling depressed, not you. I've just broken up with the nicest guy I've met in months, maybe years . . ."

"Maybe a lifetime," Sue said, eating a chip.

LINDA ignored her. "He just went cool on me. The first few times we went out were, well, fantastic. Then he seemed to switch off.

"And then last night he said he was sorry but he didn't think things were working out between us. Just like that.

"I do feel bad, Sue. I've never been given up by a boy before."

"I have," Sue said.

"But then they weren't what you might call deep romantic attachments. I mostly attract spotty gropers."

Right Boy One Day...

A Jackie short story by Jo Reade.

"Oh, you'll meet the right boy one day," Linda said. "You wait and see."

On her way home on the bus Sue started thinking about how Martin might realise that he'd made a mistake.

He'd turn up with a huge bunch of flowers and take her in his arms and whisper words of love in her ear and tell her how sorry he was to have made her sad. And she'd forgive him.

"No," Sue said. "Linda would forgive him, not me."

The bus conductor said, "Pardon?" and Sue got off the bus two stops early out of embarrassment.

That evening she decided she'd go to the disco if she could find someone to go with, so she washed and changed and then went along to Sad Sam's Café.

A lot of girls she knew went to Sad Sam's before going on to the disco. She could go with them. Only this particular evening none of them turned up.

The only person who did turn up was Martin.

She saw him come in but pretended she hadn't. She stared hard at her glass of Coke as if it was the most interesting thing in the world.

The last thing she wanted to do was talk to Martin after what he'd done to Linda. Besides, he probably wouldn't want to talk to her, anyway.

She doubted if he'd even remember her name.

She didn't look up even when he slid into the seat opposite her — not until he said, "Hi, Sue."

Then she looked up, pretending surprise. "Oh, hello, er, Martin."

He looked away and stared at her Coke glass. *Perhaps there is something interesting about that glass,* she thought.

"You know Linda and I have broken up?" he asked.

"Yes," she said.

"Does she . . . does she feel bad about it?"

"Yes," Sue said, looking at him, liking the shine of his dark hair and the way his eyebrows were shaped. *He's even got good-looking eyebrows!* she thought.

"I didn't mean to hurt her," he said. "I feel pretty bad myself."

"Eyebrows," Sue said. "I mean, why don't you give it another try? Get back together again."

"No," he said. "It wouldn't work, Sue."

"Linda would like to give it a try," Sue said.

Martin shook his head. "No."

HE looked at her. His eyes were light brown and gorgeous. Sue looked down at the interesting Coke glass. She wished he'd stop being so gorgeous for a minute so that she could think straight.

"I had a reason for giving her up," he said.

"Oh," Sue said. "Another girl?"

She felt very sad suddenly, thinking about this other girl who had come between Linda and the Course of True Love.

"Yes," he said. "You."

Sue's hand jerked and the interesting Coke glass fell to the floor. Martin picked it up. It wasn't broken.

He put it back on the table and Sue stared at it again.

"I'm not sure I heard that last bit," she said to the glass.

Her heart seemed to be beating too fast. She wondered vaguely if seventeen was a dangerous age for heart attacks, and crossed her fingers under the table.

This didn't seem like a good time to die.

"You," he said. "Don't ask me why."

"Why?" she asked.

"Let's get out of here," Martin said. "I'm coming over in a hot flush."

"So am I," Sue said.

They went out and walked up the street. Then Martin said, "I didn't come looking for you tonight, Sue. I didn't know you were going to be in Sad Sam's."

"Oh," she said.

"I wasn't going to look for you for a week."

"Oh," she said.

"It wouldn't have been fair to Linda."

THEY were silent again. Sue wondered if maybe Martin was incredibly short-sighted and had got her mixed up with a beautiful girl who was also called Sue. But as he didn't walk into any lamp-posts she decided he probably wasn't.

They walked into the park and along a path under the trees.

"I'm doing this all wrong," Martin said at last. "I don't even know if . . ."

"If what?" Sue asked.

"If you're interested. In me, I mean. I don't even know if you've really noticed me."

"I noticed you," Sue said.

"The first time I saw you," Martin said.

"I just . . . wanted to get to know you. But I was with Linda."

I've got to be dreaming this, Sue thought. *Next thing I know I'll wake up.*

"I had to break with her," Martin went on, "but I couldn't tell her why, could I?"

"Couldn't you?" Sue said.

"I couldn't tell her I was giving her up because I'd seen another girl."

He stopped and turned to Sue. She looked up at his hair, his eyebrows, his eyes, his nose, his mouth and wished her heart would stop beating so hard.

If I wake up now, she thought, *I'll never forgive myself.*

"But Linda's beautiful," she said.

"Yes, she is. So are you, in a different way.

"What's that got to do with it?"

"You don't wear glasses, do you?"

"No. Why?"

She felt herself smiling.

"No reason."

"Am I making a fool of myself, chasing you?" he asked. "Have you got another guy? Do you even like me?"

"No, no and yes," she said. "In that order."

Then he smiled and sort of relaxed. "And do I get to see you again?"

"Yes," she said. "Oh, yes, Martin."

He leaned forward very slowly and kissed her on the lips. It was a beautiful kiss.

He put his arms round her and they kissed again.

"But, Martin," she whispered. "What about Linda? It wouldn't be fair. She's all hung up about losing you."

"That's why I wasn't going to come looking for you for a week," Martin said. "So it wouldn't look so bad to her."

"I feel ever so guilty," Sue said.

"Don't. It's not your fault."

"I do, though," she said. "Like I've taken you away from her. Poor Linda."

"Oh, I don't think she'll stay broken hearted for long," he said. "Linda's not like that."

"Still," Sue said. "We'd better not meet for a week at least."

"It'll be a long week, Sue."

"That's just what I was thinking," she said. "But we've got to be fair to Linda."

"I'll be in Sad Sam's early every evening," he said. "If a week seems too long . . ."

They kissed again and it was even better. And then they said goodbye and goodnight and kissed again, and again, and again, and finally managed to let go of each other.

And Sue walked slowly home, feeling sad for Linda and glad for herself, and thinking about Martin and his good-looking eyebrows.

In her bedroom she stared hard at herself in the mirror.

"He thinks you're beautiful," she said, "and he's not even short sighted!"

It made her almost *feel* beautiful, just thinking about it.

"And he's not even a spotty groper," she told her reflection, "he's gorgeous and nice and he gave Linda up for me!"

WHEN she arrived at work next morning, feeling a bit nervous about Linda, the first thing she noticed was Linda's smile. There it was!

"You're smiling," Sue said.

"Yes," Linda smiled. "I got to thinking about me and Martin. I mean, we had a good time together but when a thing's over — it's over.

"So I went to the disco last night — and guess what?"

"What?"

"I met a boy there. His name's Peter and he's lovely, Sue, he really is."

"I'm glad," Sue said, and meant it. "I'm glad you don't feel too bad about Martin, because . . ."

Sue swallowed. "Because he's asked me to go out with him."

Linda's smile stayed on. "Oh, Sue! Didn't I tell you you'd meet the right boy one day? He's nice, Sue. You'll make a lovely pair."

Sue blinked. "You don't mind?"

"No," Linda said. "What would be the use? I wasn't really his type, that was the trouble.

"Of course I don't mind. I'm happy for you."

"Thanks, Linda," Sue said.

Mrs Barden came in at that moment and Sue went to her desk and started typing more invoices to Messrs. Martin with Love.

And Linda watched her with a kind of wistful sadness and felt glad in a funny kind of way that she had taken a walk in the park the evening before and had happened to see a boy and a girl kissing . . .

HOW TO HANDLE HIM...

The first time you meet him, you'll think he's *great*, no faults, no nasty habits — in short, you'll think he's just perfect. Once you get to know him better, and you're seeing him on a regular basis, though, you're bound to uncover a few not so nice things about him. Next time his bossiness, his moodiness or his wandering hands act get too much for you to bear, don't hurl your handbag at him — instead, read on and find out how to handle him!

THE WANDERING HANDS ACT

Every boyfriend from time to time gets carried away by his feelings and this can pose problems for his girlfriend.

There's only one way to react if your boyfriend tries to go too far physically (too far being quite simply what *you* regard as too far) and that's to stop him at once.

The best thing to do is to change the mood abruptly. Break away, say, "Stop that" sharply and get out of his clutches. Make it clear you're annoyed, and make it clear right *then* that you have limits, and tell him exactly what they are. A serious talk will cool him off *wonderfully*.

THE SOULFUL LOOK IN THE EYES ACT

If he's really nuts about you, you might begin to feel pressurised to spend all your time with him and to reassure him constantly that you really care.

If this is the case, it's very important to break away from his clutches *before* you begin to find him a drag and all the good things about your relationship fade into the past.

Tell him straight that you don't want to get too serious too soon.

Make a point of going out without him (with girl-friends maybe) at least a couple of times a week. If he moans and complains about it — well, you might even have to start thinking about ending the relationship.

THE I WANT TO BE FREE ACT

Some boys get attacks of restlessness. He might be fed up with his job or his school, or horror of horrors, he may be feeling a bit cooped up in his relationship with *you*.

His restlessness might show itself in depression, or in attacks of rather weird aggressive behaviour: playing around and doing stupid things, maybe even getting into trouble of some sort. If he's generally restless — that is, he's just fed up with life in general — all you can do is try to get him to talk about it in order to sort out some practical action.

If he's restless about his relationship with you, however, you can do more. Don't cling on for dear life, however panicked you are.

If you desperately want to keep him, the natural reaction is to say how much you love him and to beg and plead with him not to give you up. But the best thing to do is actually the opposite.

Play it *cool*. Go out without him sometimes. Don't keep ringing him up. Give the impression that you're having a great time and that you certainly don't depend on *him*.

That'll give him a chance to feel free and unhassled — and the chances are that he'll then realise how much he does like you!

THE I DON'T CARE ABOUT YOU ACT

Carelessness can show in many ways. Maybe he says he'll phone you at a certain time and then doesn't bother or forgets? Or he borrows money from you and that's the last you hear of it? Or he's careless with things that belong to you?

The best way to treat this nasty situation is to give him a short, sharp talking-to. Tell him you're fed up being taken for granted, that he's getting so don't-care in his attitude that you're sure it's best to pack it all in and finish with each other.

There's just the *chance* that he'll say "OK!" But if he does, he wasn't worth keeping anyway!

More likely, though, he'll realise how important you are to him and start taking care again.

So . . . whatever moods your boyfriend gets into, you ought to be able to handle them now!

Have you ever looked at a pin-up of your favourite star and wondered what was going through his or her mind at that moment? We certainly have, and we thought it'd be fun to guess just what they were thinking . . .

Fun was just what it was, so take a look and see what you think . . .

Look Who's Talking!

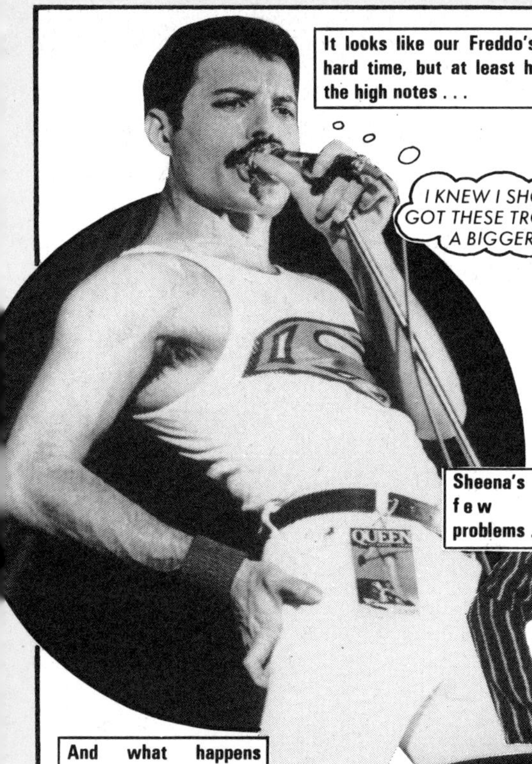

It looks like our Freddo's having a hard time, but at least he's hitting the high notes . . .

Sheena's having a few posing problems . . .

Mike Read's definitely a cool customer . . .

And what happens when the Littlest Rat meets the Biggest Rocker . . . ?

Our man in blue could show them a thing or two . . .

Just what are those pirates up to now . . . ?

Are the Specials just doing nothing . . . ?

I WAS TERRIFIED OF LOSING HIM...

MIKE was waiting for me when I left work at five o'clock. It had been my first day on the make-up counter and I was absolutely shattered. But seeing him there, his hands thrust in his pockets and his jacket pulled tightly round him to keep out the cold soon made me forget how tired I really was.

Lyn, who'd been showing me the ropes, eyed Mike as I waved.

"So that's your boyfriend, is it?" she said quietly.

I nodded and tried not to notice the surprise in her voice, but it was there all the same. It had been exactly the same at school.

Well, Mike was incredibly good-looking and I suppose no-one could understand why, out of all the girls in our year, he should have chosen me.

I mean, there's nothing wrong with me, but there's just nothing special, that's all. I've always been really shy and I hate scenes or arguments and I know that most people think that I'm a bit wet and I'd even begun to think so too, but that was before I met Mike.

Even now I still panic when I think back to my first date with him. In fact, I almost didn't go at all and spent hours trying to decide what to wear.

Everything I owned made me look like a twelve year old who'd been kitted out in Oxfam rejects and I felt sure he'd die when he saw me out of school uniform.

But somehow things didn't turn out like that at all. I survived the first date, though I suppose I was too nervous to really enjoy it, but when he asked me out again I knew he was different from anyone else I'd ever known.

The next day at work Lyn started quizzing me as soon as I joined her behind the counter.

"Have a good time last night?"

I nodded. "We did some baby-sitting for Mike's sister."

"The excitement must have killed you," Lyn drawled in a fake American accent and I felt my face go red.

Lyn was pretty outspoken and I suppose in a way that I was a bit jealous of her. She was really attractive, in fact the first time I'd met her I thought she looked a little bit like Toyah.

She was really up-to-date in a way that I knew I could never be and I envied her breezy attitude towards life.

So when I told her that I was planning to go back to school after the holidays and study for my A-levels she nearly exploded.

I busied myself stacking lipsticks as she went on and on about how carelessly I dressed and even though I knew she didn't mean to be unkind she did make me feel awful. After a while what she was saying began to sink in and I couldn't help feeling that I *was* a bit of a mess.

. . . Even though I tried, I couldn't help noticing the surprise in her voice. Mike *was* really good looking and I suppose no-one could understand why, when he could have had anyone, he'd chosen me . . .

THEN at tea break she showed me some new earrings she'd bought. "They're really nice Lyn," I said truthfully, half wishing that I could wear something as nice as that. Then, as if she'd read my mind, she said I should have my ears pierced.

"I mean, you've got to make an effort if you're to keep someone as nice as Mike," she said casually.

"I do try," I said bluntly, but I knew she didn't believe me.

"Anyway, I can't help being the way I am," I went on.

"Of course you can. Look, I'll help you if you like," she smiled.

I could tell that she really meant it — she did want to help and it was true that I had a lot to learn. Anyway, it wouldn't do any harm if I did make a few changes.

I let her make an appointment for me at the jewellers and when I mentioned it to Mike later that night he smiled.

"What's wrong with your ears the way they are?" he said, pretending to take a bite out of one of them.

"The earrings are really pretty, you'll like them," I said.

"Well, if it makes you happy . . ." he grinned.

I snuggled against him. Lyn was right, I could feel it. At least Mike hadn't reached the point where he was bored with me, but if I hadn't listened to her he might have.

Thank goodness I'd learned my lesson just in time.

Over the next couple of weeks I started to experiment with make-up, too. Mike didn't say anything when I turned up for dates wearing more than my usual mascara, so I began to get more adventurous as the weeks went by.

When pay day finally arrived, Lyn dragged me down to one of the flashiest boutiques in town and helped me choose some new clothes. Finally, we decided on a glittery top, tight white trousers and a petrel blue jacket.

"Wow, you look great," she said, as I tried the whole lot on in the locker room at work.

"I hope so, this lot cost me a fortune and I've still to pay for my hairdo on Saturday," I wailed, beginning to feel a little out of my depth. Maybe it would have looked OK on Lyn, but I felt sure I just looked stupid.

"Well get him to take you somewhere special. At least you don't have to worry about him eyeing up other girls now — you'll knock him dead!"

I FELT really strange as I stood in front of the mirror on Saturday night. My hair was cut in a slick, modern style and I had to admit that it looked far better than my old style, if you could have called it a style. I'd spent ages putting on my make-up and with the new outfit I looked a completely different person.

I was almost sick with nerves while I waited for Mike to arrive. It felt like our first date all over again and in a way maybe it was. His first real date with the new me!

And sure enough when he arrived he looked at me as though he'd never seen me before in his life.

"Like it?" I said brightly and he nodded slowly and looked pretty bewildered.

"We're going to a disco," I said rummaging about in my bag for the tickets.

"A disco!" His face fell slightly. "I thought we'd just go for a walk or go round and see my sister. We . . ."

"The disco'll be great," I assured him. "Lyn and her boyfriend are going and I thought we could make up a foursome!"

At the mention of her name his face went taut and it suddenly struck me that he always went quiet when I mentioned her name — which I'd been doing a lot lately. He was really quiet, too, as we made our way to the disco and for the first time I felt the old feeling of panic stir inside me. Something wasn't right between us, I could sense it.

Maybe it was too late, maybe Lyn had been wrong and he'd gone off me already! I tried to shut the thought out of my mind and when we arrived I was determined to enjoy myself.

WE met Lyn and her boyfriend, Joey, as soon as we arrived so at least that meant no more silences. She prattled on as if she'd known Mike all her life, but as the night wore on I could tell that he wasn't enjoying himself one little bit.

When Lyn and Joey went off for a slow dance Mike caught my hand. "Come on, let's get out of here," he hissed.

"Oh, it's not that bad, I'm quite enjoying myself," I said as casually as I could, but it was no use pretending everything was all right — it wasn't. Mike's eyes narrowed and I could tell that he was struggling hard to keep his temper. Then without a word he let go of me and headed for the door.

For a moment I was too afraid to move, but as he disappeared into the darkness I suddenly came to my senses.

He was just on his way out the door when, panting, I finally caught up with him.

"What's wrong Mike?" I pleaded. "Please tell me what's changed."

"I don't know, Karen," he said slowly. "It's not me, it's you who've changed. Ever since you started work you've become a different person.

"At first I tried to pretend everything was OK, but tonight, seeing you beside Lyn, everything fell into place.

"Karen," he said softly, "you never bothered with people like her before. She's silly and shallow and all she ever thinks about is herself.

"I don't want you to be a carbon copy of her — or anyone else for that matter, I just want you to be you!"

MY shoulders started to shake and as Mike's words washed over me, gradually the truth hit me. I *had* been trying to be another Lyn.

I was so scared of losing him that I tried to hide behind a mask of make-up and fancy clothes, but Mike — dear, loving Mike had been the first to see through it.

I gulped back the tears. My mascara was running in rivers down my face and my hair was sticking out all over the place, but it didn't seem to matter now.

Lyn hadn't meant any harm, but because I'd lacked confidence I'd let her scare me into thinking that my relationship with Mike was in danger.

But as Mike pulled me into his arms any doubts I had seemed to simply fade away.

I'd come to terms at last with the fact that it was me Mike wanted, not a clone of anyone else and that I'd have to learn all over again to be myself which, when you think about it, is the easiest, most natural thing in the world . . .

It's a cold, dark, winter evening and you can choose exactly how you want to spend it. So, what would *you* do? That's the question our roving reporters asked Jackie readers in the street, and we also got in touch with some of our favourite people for their ideas, too. Here's what we found out . . .

HOW WOULD YOU SPEND A WINTER EVENING?

Sharon Robinson, Wakefield, W. Yorks.
I'm still just a kid at heart, so my idea of a perfect winter evening is lots of snow on the ground so I can go out and make a big snowman and a slide and have a snowball fight. I've been really disappointed this last winter as we've not had enough snow to make a snowmouse, let alone a snowman!

Margaret Carter, Surrey.
Once a week during the winter, my mum bakes huge batches of scones and pies. The kitchen gets really warm and cosy and it's cakes and biscuits for the freezer and the kitchen's filled with gorgeous smells.

MIDGE URE — ULTRAVOX
The only way to spend a winter evening is snuggled up in front of the TV, preferably watching old Fred Astaire movies and dreaming about summer.

KEITH CHEGWIN
It's stupid, but I like it when the weather's really bad. When it's pouring down with rain I love to put my duffel coat on and my wellies and go out for a walk. It's like being a little kid again. I must admit I get some funny looks from people when I'm splashing about, but that doesn't matter.

Anne Wilson, Angus.
I love driving along in my boyfriend's car with the heater going full blast, the windscreen wipers going and some really good music on the casette, especially when it's dark and everything looks crisp and cold.

GRAEME GARDEN
I'd eat Lancashire hotpot in front of an open fire, and watch a really old Humphrey Bogart movie on television — for preference a previously undiscovered movie because I've seen just about all the ones known at present.

TOYAH WILLCOX
I like the very late late-night movies in London because I love to walk around afterwards, when there's just no-one about, especially if it's snowing or raining, that makes it even better. It's fantastic if I can find the really old cobbled city streets after seeing a really scarey horror movie, as a lot of the late-night ones are. You can frighten yourself to death.

Jane Hodge, Leeds.
If it's not raining or snowing, I like going out with a crowd of my friends and doing whatever we feel like, but when the weather's miserable I like to cheer myself up by planning summer holidays. I get the brochures for all sorts of far-away places, and though I usually end up at Blackpool, I like to dream.

Gina Kelly, Glasgow.
My idea of a perfect winter's evening is sitting in front of a fire which is turned up full and eating a hot dinner. The television would be showing only my favourite programmes, and of course all homework would be banned.

Diane Ainswort, Wakefield, W. Yorks.
Hibernation! I hate those old cold, dark, dreary evenings that seem to last for ever . . .

NOEL EDMUNDS
Well, there's got to be the old log fire and a big armchair — I've got both of those at home so I suppose the ideal evening would be there. I'd just sit . . . and sit . . . and doze.

BENEDICT TAYLOR
Just going to a movie. I love movies and always have, they're still one of my favourite ways of spending time — and now I've got a perfect excuse. When I was out of work and had a lot of time on my hands I used to go to the pictures a lot but then feel very guilty because I wasn't doing something more constructive. Now I'm in films and television I can tell myself it's all part of my business.

MIKE READ
I'd be at home. The log fire would be going — I do have one in my house — and if it's Christmas time then a large tree is a must. Preferably, the only light should be from the Christmas tree and the fire. I'd like a lot to eat, and then I'd like a game of charades — like on "Give Us A Clue" — or, if I've got the time to get it ready, I'd write out some unusual words and we'd play "Call My Bluff."

LEWIS COLLINS
When it's freezing cold outside I couldn't imagine spending a nicer winter evening than at my local having a game of darts with the lads. That's perfection.

Marianne Lavery, Perth.
A book, my electric blanket to toast me all over and a box of toffees. It's even better with the wind and rain howling and pattering outside my window.

EDDIE KIDD
I like to stay near the fire and either watch telly or play old films on the video. Any sort of action films, really, though I've got a lot of Clint Eastwood's, the sort of thing I'd like to do myself — something with a bit of daring in it. On that sort of evening I actually wouldn't mind if I was on my own. I spend a lot of time with crowds of people when I'm on tour during the summer, though it'd be nice to have my girlfriend there.

MATTHEW WATERHOUSE
The traditional picture, doing absolutely nothing beside a log fire. It's got all the romantic associations that really appeal to me. I do prefer to be at home; from choice I don't go to very many parties because so many people are putting on an act and not being themselves.

John Ireland, Dundee.
A video with an endless stack of films, the complete set of "Fawlty Towers," a gorgeous girl to put my arm around and a roaring log fire!

TODD CARTY
If I'm staying in then what I like at the moment is to be either at my home or a friend's home and play darts or pool. Several people I know have got those little pool tables you can assemble easily at home and I'm thinking of getting one myself, they're a lot of fun. If I'm going out with a girlfriend it's most likely to be to a cinema and then for a meal — I don't go dancing very much because I'm not very good. I've got two left feet half the time.

ADAM ANT
I'd like to have a hot bath, a lovely meal with a steaming-hot cup of tea to wash it all down, settle down to watch a good TV show — and of course have some lovely company to share it all with me.

Susan Lister, Huddersfield.
I could stand any amount of cold as long as I was with my boyfriend. He always warms me up!

PETER POWELL
There's a cottage in Wales that I know very well and that's fantastic on a winter evening. It's very barren there and the grounds go right down to the sea. There's something magic about being by the sea in winter.

TIM BROOKE-TAYLOR
I like very much the moments at the end of an evening when I'm with a small group of close friends, finishing off the red wine after a good meal and then sitting back for a long, slow conversation that goes on till the small hours while we put the entire world to rights and go to bed completely satisfied.

No place for Love...

Jarl, one of the young warriors, had loved Mara for a long time . . .
WHAT ELSE CAN WE DO? ONLY THE GODS CAN HELP US DRIVE OUT THESE STRANGERS.
PERHAPS THEY ARE SENT BY THE GODS, THEN, TO PUNISH US FOR SOMETHING WE HAVE DONE.
I WOULD LIKE TO COME FACE TO FACE WITH THESE INVADERS— THEN WE WOULD SEE HOW BRAVE THEY ARE!
HOW CONFIDENTLY YOU TALK, JARL! IF YOUR ARM WERE AS QUICK AS YOUR TONGUE, YOU'D DRIVE THESE MEN AWAY SINGLE-HANDED!
DON'T MOCK ME, MARA! I WILL NOT HAVE MY BRIDE LAUGHING AT ME!
I AM NOT YOURS YET, JARL—I HAVE THE RIGHT TO CHOOSE MY OWN HUSBAND AND I WILL PLEASE MYSELF, NOT YOU!
And suddenly, Jarl's face grew cruel and mocking . . .
WE WILL SEE, MARA. IN TIME YOU'LL KNOW THAT I'M RIGHT . . .
OH, JARL! THE TIME WAS WHEN I COULD HAVE LOVED YOU, BUT NOW . . .
Mara wandered far out of the city, into the desert, deep in thought . . .
I CAN'T UNDERSTAND MYSELF. EVERYTHING AND EVERYONE CLOSEST TO ME SEEM SUDDENLY TO HAVE BECOME LIKE STRANGERS! EVEN MY FATHER AND JARL . . .
WHAT'S THAT? OH, SOMEONE'S COMING— THEY MUSTN'T FIND ME HERE! MY FATHER WOULD BE ANGRY, IF HE KNEW I'D COME SO FAR . . .
But it was a small party—of Spanish soldiers . . .
THE INVADERS! HOW STRANGE THEY LOOK! I'VE NEVER SEEN ANYONE LIKE THEM . . . I WONDER WHAT THEY'RE DOING SO CLOSE TO THE CITY WHEN THERE ARE SO FEW OF THEM . . ?
THANK GOD WE HAVE FOUND WATER AT LAST! RIDE BACK TO THE CAMP AND INFORM THE GENERAL—I'LL STAY HERE AND WAIT.
The leader turned his back and Mara tried to creep away . . .
HE MUSTN'T SEE ME! I HAVE HEARD SO MANY TALES OF THESE MEN— IF HE CATCHES ME, HE'LL KILL ME, I KNOW IT!
Mara inched her way along the rock, but . . .
OH NO! WHERE CAN I RUN? THERE'S NO COVER HERE AND IT IS SO FAR BACK TO THE CITY! HE'S BOUND TO CATCH UP . . .
HEY—YOU THERE! STOP!

She ran for her life, but . . .
AAH! A COUGAR! IF IT ATTACKS ME—OH, IT'S GOING TO SPRING!
But the Spaniard had heard her screams, and . . .
GET BACK—STAY BEHIND ME!
And before long, the soldier's sword found its mark, but . . .
OH, LOOK OUT—ITS CLAWS—LOOK OUT!
But it was too late . . .
WHAT SHALL I DO? HE'S WOUNDED VERY BADLY—HE'LL DIE IF I LEAVE HIM HERE. I'LL HAVE TO TAKE HIM BACK TO THE CITY WITH ME—IF HIS MEN COME BACK AND FIND ME, THEY'LL KILL ME!
I HOPE I'M DOING THE RIGHT THING. ONCE I HAVE TOLD THEM THAT HE SAVED MY LIFE, SURELY HE WILL BE SAFE . . .
But when she reached the city gates . . .
LOOK—IT IS PRINCESS MARA. AND SHE HAS A STRANGER WITH HER!
ONE OF THE DEVILS FROM ACROSS THE SEA!
It was worse than she had feared . . .
A FINE PRIZE, MARA—YOU SHOULD HAVE KILLED HIM WHEN YOU HAD THE CHANCE, BUT I WILL FINISH THE JOB FOR YOU!
NO—HE SAVED MY LIFE, I OWE HIM A DEBT!
And then . . .
STOP! THE STRANGER MUST NOT DIE YET! HE MUT BE GIVEN THE BEST OF CARF- OR HE WILL NOT BE A FIT SACRIFICE TO OFFER TO THE GODS!
NO, YOU CANNOT!
IT IS A SIGN FROM THE GODS, MY CHILD. LOOK AFTER HIM WELL—HE MUST BE READY TO FACE THE KNIFE!
HE SAVED MY LIFE AND IN RETURN I'VE BROUGHT HIM HERE TO DIE! HE IS SO YOUNG—NOT MUCH OLDER THAN I AM—AND NOTHING LIKE THE STORIES I HAD HEARD . . .

IT SEEMS SO UNFAIR, SOMEHOW, THAT HE SHOULD BE KILLED— AND FOR NOTHING! I DON'T EVEN KNOW HIS NAME . . .
But Jarl had noticed her distress and was suspicious . . .
YOU'RE A VERY GOOD NURSE, MARA—AND TO A FOREIGN ENEMY, ESPECIALLY!
I'M ONLY FOLLOWING MY FATHER'S ORDERS, JARL. THE PRISONER IS TO BE SACRIFICED, AS YOU WELL KNOW!
And as the days passed . . .
THANK YOU—YOU ARE VERY KIND TO ME!
I DID NOT EXPECT YOU TO KNOW MY LANGUAGE, MIGUEL— I COULD NEVER LEARN YOURS. IT SOUNDS SO STRANGE.
I HAVE BEEN IN MEXICO NEARLY A YEAR, MARA, AND HAVE SPOKEN WITH MANY OF YOUR PEOPLE. EVERYONE HAS BEEN SO GOOD TO ME HERE, TOO— AND I AN ENEMY!
OH MIGUEL, YOU DON'T KNOW WHAT YOU'RE SAYING! HOW CAN I TELL TELL YOU THAT YOU ARE TO DIE?
And, all too soon . . .
I FEEL SO MUCH BETTER, MARA. I'M GLAD YOU'VE SHOWN ME SOMETHING OF YOUR CITY. BUT THE TEMPLE IS STRANGE TO ME—IN MY LAND, WE HAVE ONLY ONE GOD . . .
AND DO YOU NOT BUILD GREAT TEMPLES TO HIM AND WORSHIP HIM?
YES —OUR REASON FOR COMING HERE WAS TO SPREAD NEWS OF OUR GOD. BUT THE MEN HAVE BEEN CARRIED AWAY BY GREED AND CRUELTY. ALL THEY SEEK IS GOLD AND RICHES—AND THEY WILL MURDER TO GET THEM!
DO YOU WISH YOU WERE BACK IN SPAIN, THEN, WITH THOSE YOU LOVE— AND WHO LOVE YOU?
I-I DON'T KNOW, MARA . . .
THERE IS A GIRL IN SPAIN WHO PROMISED TO WAIT FOR ME. BUT WHEN YOU'RE BESIDE ME, SHE SEEMS SO FAR AWAY— IN A DIFFERENT WORLD, ALMOST . . .
And . . .
OH MIGUEL, I LOVE YOU! I LOVE YOU SO MUCH!
But still Jarl would not leave her alone . . .
I THINK YOU'RE DOING A LITTLE MORE THAN YOUR DUTY, MARA. YOUR FATHER WOULD BE VERY INTERESTED TO KNOW ABOUT WHAT'S GOING ON BETWEEN YOU AND THAT FOREIGNER!
GO AHEAD AND TELL HIM THEN, JARL. IT'S MY WORD AGAINST YOURS, REMEMBER. I WONDER WHICH OF US HE'D CHOOSE TO BELIEVE!

Mara knew she had to warn Miguel, but . . .
YOU MUST LEAVE NOW, MIGUEL—BEFORE IT'S TOO LATE! YOU CAN GET OUT TONIGHT, IF I HELP YOU . . .
WHAT ARE YOU TALKING ABOUT, MARA? I DON'T UNDERSTAND!
But already it was too late . . .
IT IS TIME, MARA. LET THE STRANGER BE PREPARED FOR SACRIFICE!
NO, FATHER—I BEG YOU!
YOU KNEW! YOU KNEW ALL ALONG THAT I WAS TO DIE—YET YOU STILL PRETENDED TO LOVE ME!
OH MIGUEL, I DO LOVE YOU! IF ONLY THERE WERE A WAY TO PROVE THAT . . .
And, as the ceremony began . . .
OH GREAT GOD, LOOK DOWN ON US AND ACCEPT THIS—
NO—NO! YOU CAN'T KILL HIM! I WON'T LET YOU!
I AM A PRINCESS OF THE AZTEC PEOPLES. IT IS MY RIGHT TO CLAIM ANY MAN I WISH FOR MY HUSBAND, AND I CHOOSE HIM!
IT IS YOUR RIGHT, MARA—BUT YOU RISK THE WRATH OF THE GODS!
I CARE NOTHING FOR THE GODS!
IF ANY HARM COMES TO US BECAUSE OF THIS MARA, YOU WILL BE RESPONSIBLE—AND YOU WILL BOTH BE PUNISHED!
YOU NEED NOT WORRY—WE CANNOT STAY HERE! YOU WILL NEVER HAVE TO SET EYES ON EITHER OF US AGAIN!
YOU'RE SAFE NOW MIGUEL—THEY CAN'T TOUCH YOU.
THANKS TO YOU, MARA, BUT I THINK WE HAD BETTER GO. YOUR JARL HAS MURDER IN HIS EYES!
AND NOW WE ARE BOTH OUTCAST AND ALONE. I DON'T KNOW WHAT WILL BECOME OF US—BUT AT LEAST WE WILL BE TOGETHER.
And so they journeyed for many hours, until . . .
OH MIGUEL, YOU'VE HARDLY SPOKEN TO ME SINCE SUNRISE! WHAT'S WRONG? OH, I WISH I WERE NOT SO TIRED . . .
WE'RE BOTH TIRED, MARA . . .

DO YOU WISH YOU HAD NOT COME WITH ME, THEN? YOU WOULD HAVE DIED WITHOUT ME!
OH MARA, I LOVE YOU BUT—I CANNOT STAY HERE FOR THE REST OF MY LIFE!
I MUST RETURN TO SPAIN SOME DAY, MARA—IT'S MY HOME!
OH MIGUEL, PLEASE—DON'T LEAVE ME!
But then . . .
LOOK! SMOKE—FROM THE CITY!
COME ON! WE MUST GET BACK!
But by the time they reached it . . .
IT'S IN RUINS—THE WHOLE PLACE! WHAT'S HAPPENED—WHERE IS EVERYONE?
And then, from the wreckage . . .
IT'S JARL! JARL, WHAT HAPPENED? WHAT WAS IT?
THE INVADERS—THEY CAME FROM NOWHERE, KILLING AND PLUNDERING!
EVERYONE IS DEAD—YOUR OWN FATHER TOO, MARA, BECAUSE YOU CHEATED THE GODS OF THEIR SACRIFICE. THIS IS YOUR DOING!
JARL, I SWEAR TO YOU—
THE GODS WILL NOT BE CHEATED AGAIN—THIS TIME THERE WILL BE NO SECOND CHANCE, FOREIGNER!
NO, JARL—NO!
And Mara threw herself in front of Miguel as the spear arched forward . . .
MARA—OH MARA, MY LOVE . . .
YOU WON'T LEAVE ME, WILL YOU, MIGUEL? YOU WON'T GO BACK TO SPAIN AND LEAVE ME ALL ALONE?
NEVER, MY LOVE, I'LL STAY WITH YOU FOREVER . . .
OH, MIGUEL . . .
But it was too late . . .
OH, MARA, WE WERE TOGETHER SUCH A SHORT TIME, AND NOW YOU ARE DEAD, I HAVE NOT THE HEART TO GO HOME. BUT I WILL NEVER FORGET YOU, MY DARLING—NEVER . . .
THE END

YOUR JACKIE POP-A-CROSS

ACROSS

1. Top TV programme about a school (6, 4).
3. The Stewart tartan terror (3).
4. Also known as Graham McPherson (5).
6. ---- Peter (4).
7. She's a Modern Girl (6).
10. Initially a Superman (1, 1).
12. Ranking Roger's lot (4).
13. --- Sedaka or Christopher ---- (4).
14. Saturday is ------ day! (6).

DOWN

1. Numan or Glitter (4).
2. This man in blue has a seasonal surname (4).
5. Founders of 2-Tone (8).
7. Insect bite that a lot of us would love to have! (5).
8. Presley or Costello (5).
9. "--- of Spades." Motorhead hit (3).
11. Irish rodents (3).

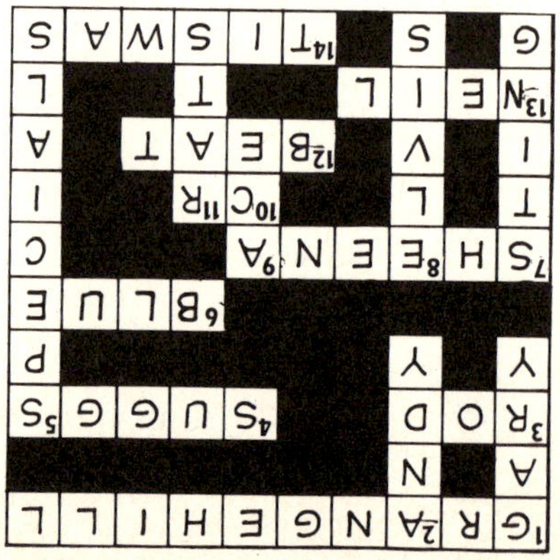

When you meet someone for the first time you need all the clues you can to help you get things going. The easiest way to assess someone's character is, quite simply, to look them straight in the face — it's that easy!
Have a look at our Jackie guide to the face shapes below and make sure you're prepared next time you meet someone new . . .

FACE THE FACTS!

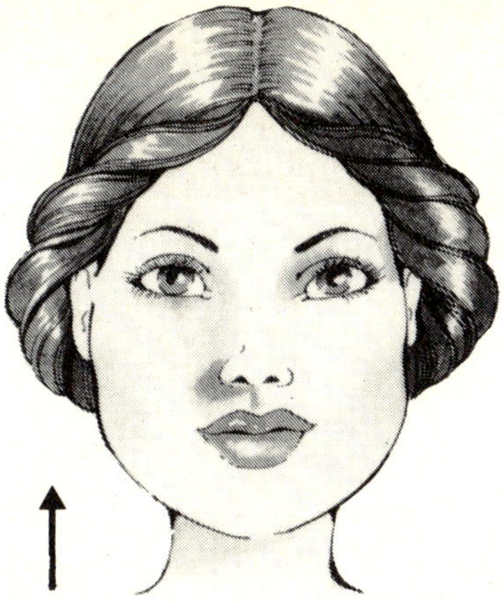

Pear
This is a slightly nervous character who has a tendency to shrink back and let other people take over and run her life. Very often there is an interest in creating things — from pottery to food. She is warm, loving and kind, with a friendly and modest nature.

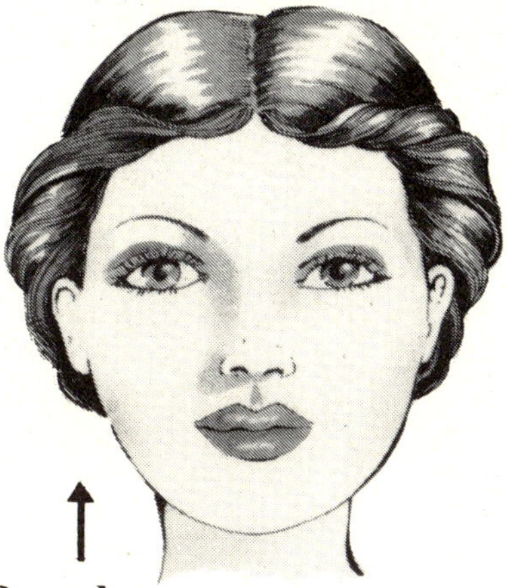

Round
This shape of face belongs to a pleasure-loving and fun-seeking person who thrives on variety and change. She'll be easily pleased but just as easily hurt, because she'll rush into new romantic situations without thinking. She's always full of enthusiasm for new ideas, schemes and plans, whether romantic or otherwise.

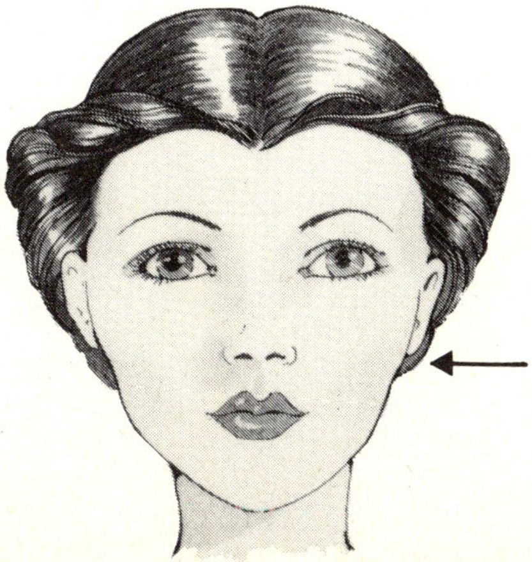

Oval
The dreamers and the hopelessly romantic all have oval-shaped faces. They tend to be sensitive and highly strung, which means they're easily annoyed. This shape of face shows a character who needs attention and admiration. She tends to be idealistic about romance and is rather in love with love.

Square
This is a bossy type, although dependable and reliable as a friend. However, she always wants to lead rather than follow and enjoys getting her own way. She has strong will-power and so ends up being the dominant person in any organisation. She can't stand being ordered about or made to feel small.

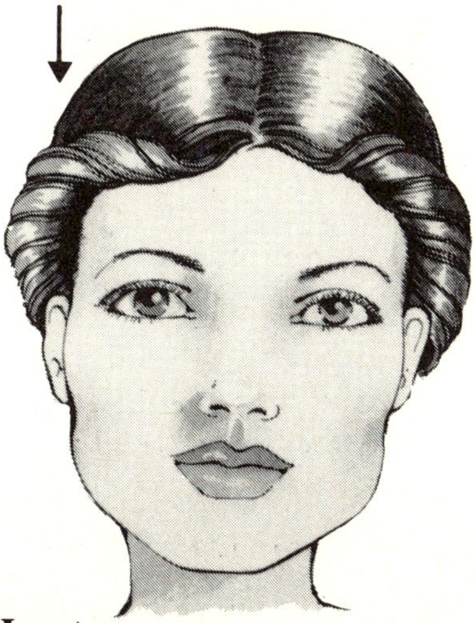

Heart
This face maybe looks really soft but, in fact, there's usually a very hard and determined nature behind it with a strong character. She's usually extremely affectionate and will have a well-developed, possibly off-beat, sense of humour. She'll be good fun to be with and rarely gets annoyed enough to hold a grudge.

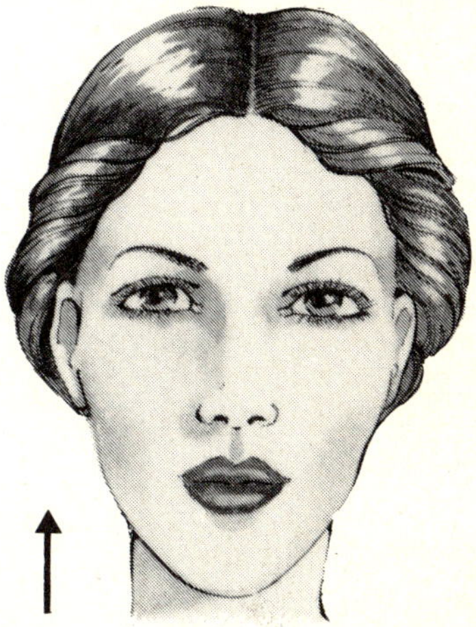

Long
This face reveals a forceful character who likes nothing better than to be physically active. She's always moving around and generally doing everything at the double. Usually with plenty of push and drive, she'll always be in a hurry to get things done and can't wait for tomorrow to come. She'll tend to make very quick decisions where affairs of the heart are concerned.

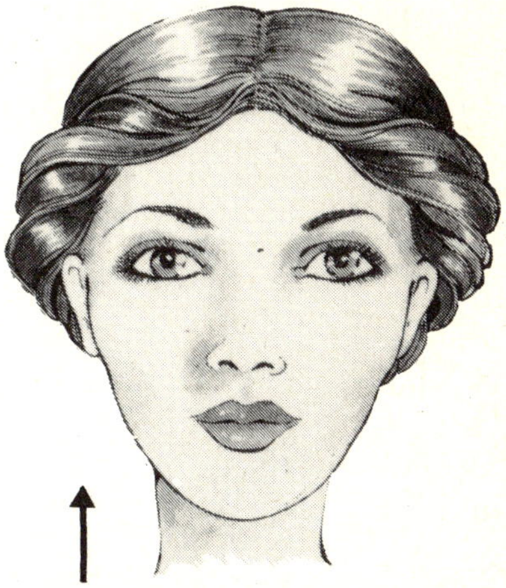

Triangular
Easy going, lovable and just a tiny bit lazy, that's what this shape of face reveals. Her nature is affectionate but she doesn't like making an effort in anything. Being loved and looked after appeals to her and it's very rare for this shape of face to become aggressive or anti-social in any way. Anything for a quiet life, that's this one.

Remember that although we've used girls' faces here, the shapes and rules also apply to boys. So, get out there and get looking for your ace-face!

DESERT ISLAND DELIGHTS

Look at Gary Numan's eyes (OK, OK, ten minutes is enough!). Now, examine Sting's mouth very, *very* closely. Next, cast your expert eye over Phil Lynott's beautiful bone structure . . .

All of the famous faces you see here are more than just pretty, they're character revealing! We asked an expert to analyse all these famous faces and here are her findings. To make it just that little bit more fun, we asked her to tell us how they'd cope on a desert island. Compare our expert's findings to the faces of the people in *your* life, your boyfriend's especially — we guarantee you'll be amazed!

STING

Sting would most definitely hate living on an island! His large forehead reveals his highly active mind and also his need to be where the action is. The slightly wiry hair and thick eyebrows show that he has a nasty temper when crossed, and that he likes to travel rather than remain in one place for very long.

His determined chin and widely spaced mouth, with the lower lip slightly fuller than his top lip are all signs of an affectionate and loving nature (he probably loves to flirt!). His ears are set well back on his head, showing that he can make quick decisions when necessary – and one of them would probably be to get off his island as quickly as possible as he would miss his wife a lot!

GARY

Gary has a broad, deep forehead which means he's a lover of freedom and movement, so the prospect of being stuck on an island wouldn't exactly wow him at first! He'd be reasonably adaptable on an island as he's a bit of a loner anyway, and doesn't mind his own company.

His deep set eyes and the way they turn down a little at the outside corners reveal his extreme sensitivity and maybe even irritability under pressure. His well formed, firm mouth is a sign of strength of character and a strong will, and also of a passionate, affectionate personality who's attractive to the opposite sex. (We wouldn't argue with that!)

On the whole, Gary would probably cope well with island life.

PHIL

Phil has a long, rather narrow face which indicates a forceful personality. He'd probably cope quite well on an island. His eyes have slightly drooping lids which is a sign of a very affectionate nature, and an ardent temperament when in love.

The thin nose and small mouth reveal a tendency to jealousy. As these features also indicate plenty of intuition, it would be difficult to fool him if you were to two-time him! His long chin shows that he's a strong, active and energetic character, someone who'd be quite happy fending for himself on his island, but who would miss company – female company especially!

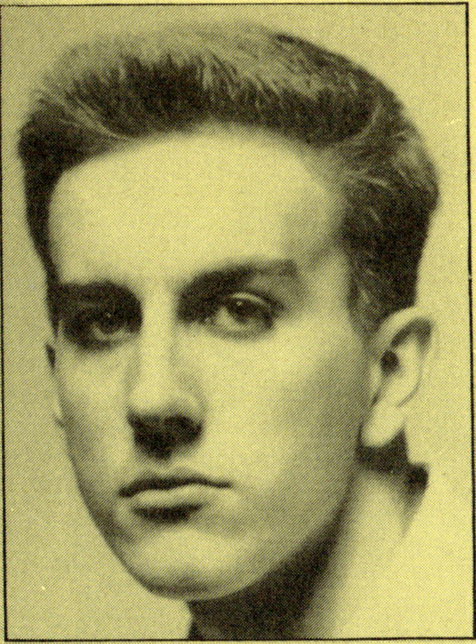

TERRY (Specials)

Terry's wide forehead and the way his face tapers down, narrowing towards his chin, reveals his tendency to brood. Being left alone on a desert island might make him even more broody, so it's doubtful he'd be over the moon at the prospect of living on a desert island.

He's probably a very changeable character in his moods and he'd have lots of up and down days. His deep set eyes indicate strong physical energy, and a mind that thinks a lot. He would be cautious, capable, and constructive. The fact that his ears stick out a little from the side of his head reveals he'd have difficulty in keeping to any sort of routine on his enforced exile.

His mouth is generous and wide, showing a friendly, affectionate nature, and this is confirmed by his lower lip protruding forward (a sign of an ardent and passionate nature!). In other words, he'd get a little bit lonely if he did have to live on an island by himself!

MICHAEL

Michael is shy and this is revealed in the way his mouth turns up a little at the corners. He wouldn't enjoy the solitude of living on an island but his large, dreamy eyes would seem to indicate he isn't practical enough to build himself a raft or boat to escape on, unfortunately!

His wide eyes and the tiny rolls of fat underneath them indicates a romantic and highly sensitive nature. His heart-shaped face and slightly squarish chin reveal a passionate and tender personality with a need to love and be loved.

Michael's much too nice a person to be left all alone on a desert island, even a beautiful one – he'd hate it!

JIMMY

Jimmy would soon try to escape from an island and this shows in his round, sociable face, the way his mouth curls slightly at the corners, and the broad nose. All in all, Jimmy wouldn't be too keen on solitude.

His pointed chin shows him to be a thinker with good imagination, so if he did find himself stranded on an island he'd soon have a shelter up, and a supply of food and water laid on. He needs to express his personality, though – preferably before an audience – and this would cause him to dislike being alone for too long.

His eyes are spaced far apart revealing an emotional nature, a sense of humour and a caring, loving temperament.

THE DO's & DONT's OF *Babysitting!*

Babysitting can be a great thing if you want to earn some spare cash, but anyone who's done it before will tell you that it can also be one of the most gruesome experiences around! The dangers aren't always obvious, either — everyone knows that babies cry a lot and have a habit of bringing up milk before it's had a chance to get to their little tums, not to mention doing nasty things in their nappies! But there are other sides to babysitting which are *guaranteed* to leave you a nervous wreck. So to avoid any disasters, just follow our fun guide to the do's and don'ts of babysitting . . .

DO be prepared! Get dressed in your old jeans and even older shirt, and practise the art of holding your breath and counting to ten before you lose your temper — before you start asking silly questions like "*Why?*", just imagine how you'll feel in four hours' time when Junior is hanging from your hair, screaming in your ear and trying to push a mushy banana down the back of your neck.

A few bedtime stories and well-rehearsed lullabies always make things easier, and if you're very smart *and* have a cassette-recorder, you'll be able to arrange it so that you can croon baby to sleep *and* watch "Dallas" at the same time . . .

DON'T spend hours in front of the mirror putting your face on before you leave, even if baby's dad *is* your history teacher who looks exactly like Sting. For one thing, the average hello/goodbye routine lasts for thirty seconds, before Dad shoots off with his wife (who's even better at putting on make-up than you, anyway) — and for another, you'll realise it was all a waste of time when your face is smeared in rusks, chocolate, Vaseline and the aforesaid mushy banana.

There's not much point in bringing along a book or knitting either, as babies have a habit of chewing and dribbling over baby-sitters' most prized possessions. And whatever you do, don't decide this is the perfect time to practise doing up your nails. Nail polish and remover don't really agree with valuable antique furniture, and any-way — Mum might not be too happy to discover that her little darling has suddenly developed scarlet nails . . .

DO put your foot down (preferably not actually *on* the baby!) when it comes to games. When it's almost midnight and you've been playing Bucking Broncos since seven, it's time to carry Junior off to bed, screaming — and that's you, not the baby! You've got to let the little devil know who's boss.

Good games to play are "Who Can Keep Quiet The Longest" (especially if you've remembered your tranny and ear-plug — babies don't tend to understand things like that), and "Holding Your Breath" — there's no way baby can win with his tiny little lungs, and with any luck, all that lack of oxygen will make him feel sleepy . . .

DON'T start any game which baby loves so much he'll never let you stop, such as Bucking Broncos (but if you do, make sure baby can take your weight before you start!). Another game to be avoided at all costs is the Indian War Game. It almost always ends with the brave Apache (him) tying the bad cowboy (you) to the totem pole (chair). Playing Houdini, the great escapologist, is OK if your name's Houdini, but not so much fun if you're just plain old you who can't even get out of your jeans without a fight, let alone sixty feet of knotted string.

Above all remember that the whole point of playing games is to get baby so exhausted that you can have some peace — so you can forget about learning games, intellectual stimulation and child psych-ology. After all, teachers get paid a lot more than babysitters . . .

DO check with baby's parents that it's OK, before you invite your boyfriend round to keep you company. After all, it's not your house and it's only manners to find out whether or not they object. Make sure your boyfriend knows what's involved, too — it could be the end of a beautiful friendship if he spends the whole time hiding in the upstairs loo with his fingers in his ears muttering "Why me? Why me . . ?"

DON'T let Mum and Dad come home to find the two of you rolling on the Axminster having a good time. They'll never believe you when you tell them you were looking for a lost nappy pin. Even worse, don't let them come home to find a party in full swing — that really *is* unforgiveable! Don't let your boyfriend raid the cigar box or the booze cupboard, even if there's only a can of shandy left, or it'll be all round the neighbourhood that you're going out with a sticky-fingered alcoholic.

DO your best — that's all you can do. Babies are wet quite a lot of the time, and if you had a wet nappy, you'd cry, too. If you don't know how to change a nappy, then tell Mum before she goes off to her cocktail party/ horror movie /dinner with her be-loved's boss . . . it's only fair. She'll either tell you exactly what to do, or wonder why she bothered to ask you to babysit in the first place.

If you *do* decide to change the baby (no, we don't mean swop him for a box of chocs!), then be careful with pins — they can do an awful lot of harm. It *is* possible to tie on a nappy without using pins, but if in doubt, then just make sure you cover the most im-portant parts. If you can't work out what those are, you probably need a babysitter yourself!

DON'T pinch baby's sweets and choco-late. Apart from the fact that this is mean because he's too little to fight back, they might come in handy later on as bribes. Don't help yourself to anything which hasn't been left out for you — unless you've been told to, of course. Don't leave crumbs all over the Axminster either — if you've made a mess, it's up to you to clear it up.

And whatever you do, *don't* ever, ever nip out just for a few minutes to the chip shop or the Chinese takeaway! When it comes to baby's bottle, make sure it's not too hot or you'll have a very cross red-gummed baby to deal with. If he's on to solids, don't ram the spoon in so hard it nearly comes out of his nappy — and don't bounce him up and down afterwards. He'll be sick — all over you!

Finally don't assume that you have to spend every second looking anxiously at baby to see if he's all right. Some babies actually *do* sleep all night, and there's a good chance that the two of you will be able to curl up on the couch and have a nice evening, with baby on the floor watching you happily — just so that he can tell Mum and Dad all about it when they get home . . .

Kites Of Fancy!

Be a little different this year and discover a whole new way of occupying yourself in the open. Go fly a kite!

Kites aren't just for kids, you know. It takes skill to fly one and if you can manage to make your own you'll be well pleased with your creative efforts. And the good thing is, when they're not in flight they look great as wall decorations!

First, find a kite. Toy shops should sell ready-made kites but you can make your own from soft wood for the frame, and paper, cloth or plastic as the cover. Hobby shops will supply the raw materials and plans, or look out for a kite book in your local library or bookshop.

It's difficult to plan a day to fly your kite. You'll find you have to follow the weather, and wait for a windy day. On a calm day when chimney smoke rises vertically you should be able to get a paper kite up, when there's a gentle breeze you can fly plastic kites, too, and when the wind's strong enough to blow your hat off leave your paper kite at home and fly a plastic or cloth one instead. Don't attempt to fly your kite if the wind's really gusty, though.

The best areas to fly kites are flat, open fields, beaches, empty football pitches or spacious parklands. Keep an eye out for things that could bring your kite down, such as buildings, trees and electrical or telephone wires.

Believe us, it's a great feeling that has to be shared, to watch your colourful kite soaring high in the sky, so drag along some friends, too.

PATCHWORK

Are You Worthy Of A Dog?

If you've been hoping, wishing and hinting that you'd like a little pup for Christmas, perhaps you should realise just how much time you'll need to devote to it.

As soon as your pup starts to show independence by running away from you, it's ready to be trained. This'll take about ten minutes every day and only one person in the household should train the pup to prevent it getting confused.

The best way to train a puppy is to attend dog-training classes or to follow a reliable manual.

A puppy should be basically trained after three months but an older dog may take longer.

After six months your dog will be ready to take the further step of "off the lead" training. However, one quality in *you* is absolutely essential and that is patience! So before you ask, "How much is that doggy in the window?" ask yourself, "Could I cope with a dog?"

Be A Sport

Want to feel happier, fitter and sleep more soundly in 1982? Then consider taking up a sport.

Walking can be done almost at anytime and almost anywhere. For maximum benefit wear comfortable shoes with a firm support for the arches and light, loose clothing.

If you live in the country, **cycling's** a great exercise, but remember, cycling in traffic is always potentially dangerous. Check your bike thoroughly before you take it out on the road.

Swimming properly should stretch and develop almost every part of your body. Find a steady pace in a stroke or mixture of strokes that suits you and never swim within two hours of a heavy meal or allow yourself to get so cold that cramp sets in, and stick to approved and supervised swimming pools.

Gee-Up Gloomy Evenings!

Brighten up the dull winter evenings by planning the best summer holiday you've ever had!

First, do a little ground work, though, and send away for the "Ponies Of Britain" extensive, descriptive list of approved trekking and riding centres.

For example, how do you like the sound of one centre that gives you "breathtaking views of North Cornwall's rugged coastline" as you gallop along on your pony?

Some of the centres supervise girls between 7 and 14, if you felt like going trekking on your own, while others are strictly for older riders or complete families.

If you'd like a copy of the list, write to "Ponies Of Britain," Ascot Racecourse, Ascot, Berkshire. The list costs £1.25, inclusive of postage.

CHEST A MINUTE!
Does your T-shirt

Cool For Cats

Basically you're very fashion conscious, you may well be an animal lover, too, but that's probably a secondary consideration as far as you're concerned. When you go out looking for a T-shirt you want something that's bang up to date because that's just what you are yourself, and not only as far as clothes are concerned; you enjoy anything that's new. Like new boys! You probably change boyfriends quite often but you always manage to stay friends as you're a friendly, outgoing sort of girl.

Smart Cookie

You rate brain power pretty high and if you wore this type of T-shirt most people would assume you were brainy and at Cambridge. But that wouldn't bother you as you'd just tell them that you were heading there. You've probably got your future all mapped out. You may even have your boyfriend under your thumb, too, although he won't know it. You're too smart for that!

You live life at a pretty fast pace and can't be bothered to waste time with dreamers or dum-dums. You probably can't be bothered with clothes and fashion much either and T-shirts could account for most of your wardrobe. Smart girl, they look up to date however old they are!

I'm Paula, Try Me!

OK, if your name isn't Paula there's no way you'd wear a T-shirt with Paula on it, but if it was, would you like everyone to know your name? If you would then you're a very confident, outgoing sort of girl who loves meeting, chatting and just being with people *all* the time.

Sometimes you're a little too trusting for your own good though, and could get in with a bad crowd just to avoid hanging around on your own, so try to be a little selective.

You make a great girlfriend because you're always happy and laughing — but try not to panic if the guys seem to love and leave you, it's just that they know you'll find another one very soon.

speak louder than words?

IMAGINE it's Saturday and you're downtown shopping for a new T-shirt. On entering your favourite shop you're faced with the choice here. Which would **you** buy? Your decision is vital because, as you'll read here, the T-shirt you wear makes your character quite clear!

Bikes Mean Boys!

Sporting the Isle of Man TT Road Race on your chest is bound to attract the guys. They'll want to know if you were really there, and when, and are you going this year and can they come too! Thing is, you'll be able to answer all their questions, about bikes too! You're probably one of those girls who really prefers boys' company to girls'. Fashion, make-up, dates are subjects that bore you to death but mention football, bikes or cars and your eyes light up. You may find it hard to make girlfriends because they're probably green with envy at your ability to always be surrounded by boys, but that doesn't worry you as you're too busy working out how to raise the cash to get to the Isle of Man next year!

Daydream Believer

Soon as you saw the words "Tropicana" and "Tahiti" you zeroed in on this T-shirt because just the words will have sent you into daydreams of mammoth proportions. Slight problems occur in your real life when you set eyes on a handsome hunk and immediately fall head over heels in love with him. You're not really interested in good old Fred next door. Luckily you're an optimist, though, and when you realise the dreamy hunk belongs to another you'll happily start dreaming of an imaginary Mr Perfect. Just watch out that all this dreaming doesn't mean you miss out on real life opportunities that may come your way.

Natural Nut

You're nutty but nice, because you're a simple, straightforward kind of girl. That's why you chose the simplest T-shirt of all, the one that quite simply tells the world that you like something, which in this case happens to be Madness.

Life is two tone as far as you're concerned with no in-betweens. You see no reason to beat about the bush — if you decide you like or don't like someone or something you just come straight out and say so.

And when you do like something you'll totally dedicate yourself to it. If it's a group you'll join their fan club, beg, steal or borrow any poster you can find of them and travel miles to see them. And if there's a special guy you like you'll expect to see him as often as possible and expect 100% dedication back from him!

A Jackie Quiz

What Goes On In YOUR Mind?

When you're faced with a strange or unusual situation, do you look on it as an adventure, or do you long for the security of ordinary things? The pictures here use recognisable objects, but they're put together in a way that may seem disturbing or puzzling. But if you let your imagination get to work on them, you'll be amazed at how their meaning becomes clear — and how much you've revealed about your hidden depths . . .

1. Is this jacket really as innocent as it appears to be, or is there a more sinister story behind it? Use your psychic powers to decide.

a. "It's a picture from the dream of a young man. He's been rejected by the girl he loves, and the jacket symbolises the emptiness and loneliness he feels inside. Life has no meaning for him any more — he's just an empty shell . . ."

b. "The jacket belongs to a Missing Person. The boy who ran away took all his possessions with him, but left this jacket hanging inside-out. It's the only clue to his disappearance, the only thing the police have to work on . . ."

c. "It's the image that haunts a young man who believes he's murdered someone, and the hanging jacket symbolises the person who's been killed. Did it really happen or was it all in the imagination? This is the terrible question the young man must find the answer to . . ."

2. How would you analyse this strange self-portrait?

a. "The cat symbolises Nine Lives, and the man who painted the self-portrait takes risks but feels he can look after himself. He wants to be independent and has a lot of self-confidence."

b. "The cat is a symbol of evil. The man looks ordinary on the surface, but feels he's been taken over by strange powers. He's desperately worried about himself and is terrified that he might be enslaved by black magic."

c. "The cat symbolises watchfulness. Although the man has friends and a normal social life, he doesn't trust people deep down. He tries to hide his feelings and his shyness, but is always afraid of being deceived or betrayed."

3. How on earth do you interpret *this*?

a. "It's part of a strange religious sect. They're too poor to buy shoes, anyway, but they believe that reading newspapers is a sin, so they wrap them round their feet to keep warm instead."

b. "It's an old-fashioned cure for swollen ankles! Old fish-and-chip newspaper works best. You just rub salt and vinegar into the affected part, wrap the paper round and leave on for six hours, by which time the ankles are slim and beautiful — if a bit smelly!"

c. "It's someone going to a fancy-dress party — dressed up as a tramp!"

4. This flower picture was found inside an old Bible in a disused attic. It was painted to illustrate a story, and although the picture remains, the story has been lost in the mists of time. What was it?

a. "It was a traditional fairy story. The prince had to go through many dangerous adventures, and kill many dragons, to find this rare magic flower. He had to pick the flower and put it on the princess's windowsill at dawn, before they could marry and live happily ever after."

b. "It was a ghost story called The Curse of the Black Orchid. The story tells of a girl who picks the flower because it's so unusual. But dreadful things begin to happen all around her, and she doesn't realise until it's too late, that by picking the flower she's released the soul of an evil witch, hell-bent on destroying everything in her sight."

c. "It was part of an old legend. The solitary black flower protected an isolated village from roaming wolves, bears and other hazards. But one night a traveller who had lost his way stepped on the flower and crushed it. There was a sudden and terrible landslide and the village was wiped out and lost for ever."

5. How do you react to this — and what do you think the explanation could be?

a. "It's rather intriguing — it's one of those weird exhibits at a modern art exhibition. The artist is trying to convert people to vegetarianism, because if you eat feathers, it symbolises eating a bird, like a chicken."

b. "There's something extremely menacing about it. I imagine someone has put it there as a terrible warning or omen of some kind — it's like voodoo, a prelude to something horrible which is about to happen."

c. "It seems funny to me — I think the feathers were put in the bowl by a mad aunt visiting her niece — this old lady is completely dotty and always doing crazy things like putting shoes in the fridge and vegetables on the top of the wardrobe!"

6. What is the meaning of this picture?

a. "It's a girl's vision of herself in a dream, depicting her state of mind. She looks completely lost and disorientated. Her personality is changing, she's somehow becoming a different person and she feels extremely fearful and disturbed."

b. "It's a girl doing keep-fit exercises. Well, she looks awfully pale and washed-out, poor thing. She's probably recovering from a bout of flu, and has decided to become a health fiend."

c. "It's a symbolic picture. The girl is head over heels in love and her whole world turned upside down when she met this fantastic boy in a whirlwind romance. She feels it's all like a wonderful dream and can hardly believe it's real."

Scoring.

1. (a) = 4, (b) = 2, (c) = 6.
2. (a) = 2, (b) = 6, (c) = 4.
3. (a) = 6, (b) = 4, (c) = 2.
4. (a) = 2, (b) = 6, (c) = 4.
5. (a) = 4, (b) = 6, (c) = 2.
6. (a) = 6, (b) = 2, (c) = 4.

Completely bemused? You're meant to be! Now add up your points and check with our conclusions – which should clear everything up for you . . .

Conclusions

12-19 Points:

You have a logical turn of mind and the ability to make sense out of chaos and nonsense. You're clear-headed and practical. You analyse situations calmly, reasoning everything out and not letting your emotions stand in the way of good judgment. So however strange and peculiar things appear to be, you can always use your reasoning-power and commonsense to interpret and understand.

With such a mature approach, you'll cope with life extremely well and achieve your ambitions. You won't be held back by too many fears and worries, and your sense of humour and optimistic outlook give you a great advantage. You're an active person and when you decide to go for a goal you can be extremely methodical and hard working.

You're not usually mind-boggled by anything! You're good at solving problems and you know where you're going in life.

Social life shouldn't be a problem to you, either. You're self-confident in company, meeting people naturally and making friends easily. You've the ability to get on well with boys as people, and not just in a romantic way, though when you really fall in love you can be as romantic as anyone else. You know your own feelings, and you're in control of your relationships and the world around you.

20-28 Points:

You're intrigued and fascinated by extraordinary situations and weird happenings and you can become quite carried away at times. You're a romantic at heart but you also have the ability to bring yourself down to earth and be sensible and realistic.

The imaginative side of your nature brings fun and inspiration into your life, while the realistic side helps you to cope with life's problems. You're not always very methodical in your way of thinking and analysing situations, but sometimes a mixture of reason and intuition can lead you to the right solution to a problem.

You're rather emotional, but have the ability to control your feelings when you make the effort. You sum people up instinctively. You're understanding and sympathetic and make a very good friend. You're very sensitive to other people's feelings, and can therefore get deeply involved with friends on an emotional level.

For you it's love that makes the world go round. The excitement of mad, magical romance appeals to you, but a basis of real love, sincere feeling and trust is essential. Truth is very important to you, so that although you can dream of moonlight and stardust, your relationships must be really genuine if they're to mean anything to you.

You're open-minded in your attitude to life, which means that your future should be very varied, with a wide choice of relationships and experiences.

29-36 Points:

You love being involved in weird situations and peculiar happenings, and you look for sensation and excitement. So your thoughts are often jumbled and chaotic, and your emotions confused and changeable. You react on your emotions all the time without taking trouble to plan your life.

No wonder you often get into muddles — you can be moody and depressed one minute, ecstatically happy the next. There is a tendency for you to dwell too much on the darker side of life, to exaggerate problems and work yourself up into a dreadful state about things which could be smoothed out quite easily with a bit more practical, realistic, thought and action.

But the realm of imagination is your special talent. You're fascinated by the strange and unusual and like to express the creative side of your nature.

Relationships are not always easy for you because you seem to expect others to get on to your wavelength, and you don't always make the effort to meet people halfway. Your expectations of love and romance tend to be too high, and real relationships are sometimes disappointing by comparison.

So don't lose your inspired and imaginative qualities, but do try to come down to earth a little bit in ordinary everyday life.

New Looks

TARTAN TRENDS . . .

Tartan never seems to go out of fashion — it looked good on Bonnie Prince Charlie and looks just as good 1982 style! Mix your tartans and tweeds for a really original look — add knickerbockers, waistcoats and a huge scarf slung over your shoulder — and you'll be all set for your own Highland fashion fling!

. . . or are they? If you get the feeling you've seen the new 1982 fashions before – you probably have – in your history books! This year, the designers have gone as far afield as places like Turkey and Lapland to bring you clothes with an ethnic, peasant flavour – and as far back in time as Bonnie Prince Charlie for the colourful tartans we'll be seeing a lot of. The Pirate styles are still as exciting as they were in Errol Flynn's day – and the romantics can look forward to an even frillier new year!

SWASHBUCKLING STYLE

Pirate styles are still very much part of the picture for 1982 fashion — in true Errol Flynn tradition! Look out for swashbuckling touches like sashes, billowing pants, puffy sleeves, lace-up tunics, thick gold bangles right down to fall-down socks. It all adds up to one of the most adventurous, exciting looks around!

FOLKLORE FASHION

The ethnic influence! Smocks, dirndl skirts, boleros, embroidered blouses, gaucho pants and jacquard socks are all coming back in style! Pile on the layers — not just to keep you warm! Use your imagination and mix different prints together for a really colourful peasant look!

New Looks

ROMANTIC RUFFLES

Take a chance on romance! Go for pretty, softer new styles — ruffled blouses, black velvet bows — with lots of frills and lace. The new romantic styles include knickerbockers, breeches and capes — in old-fashioned fabrics like velvet, satin and taffeta. So take a trip back in time to discover a brand-new way of romantic dressing!

Playing Around!

Some stars' talents know no bounds – here are some actors who are spare-time musicians and some musicians who love to act!

Sting's Acting Thing

Last April Sting put down his guitar and went out into the cold to act in a weird BBC production called "Artemis '81." Seen here "in training" with seasoned actor Hywel Bennett.

A Real Pro!

Has Lewis Collins discovered a new way of learning his lines by setting them to music? Who knows, he certainly looks very professional about playing the piano.

Starship Trouper

Away from the terrors of outer space, Richard Hatch likes to relax with some old-fashioned, soothing earth music . . .

On The Beat

Although he plays the hard man on screen, it's obvious Dennis Waterman is a real softie when it comes to music. Here he shows a young fan how to make a guitar "talk!"

Shaw Fingered!

Yeah, well . . . does Martin really know how to play the guitar? Maybe he's developed a new technique of one-hand strumming. If he plays as well as he looks, we're all ears!

What A Break Through

Hazel O'Connor was elevated from stage to screen when she starred in "Breaking Glass" and seemed to have little difficulty in acclimatising herself to the new set-up, especially since her leading man was dishy Jon Finch. But then outrageous Hazel's probably acting all the time, isn't she?

It's A Phil Life!

Phil Daniels combines the best of both worlds, acting *and* playing in a band. So catch him where you can — on stage, screen or gig.

What A Dream

When David's up on the screen he makes dreams come true before your very eyes. If you've seen him in "Silver Dream Racer" we bet you didn't dare blink, let alone dream, in case you missed a moment of his great acting.

Playing With Toyah

Wild Toyah Willcox is here transformed into a sedate blonde for her role in one of the "Tales Of The Unexpected." Toyah is at home both in the music and acting worlds — she's a real mistress of disguise.

From Blondie To Bored Housewife

Bored housewife? Has Debbie given up on Blondie? Never, she's just doubling up by doing the occasional film here and there. And here in particular is a shot from the film "Union City."

THE

All the things you'll find hardest to understand about your boyfriend, and the things he's most worried about, are all here. If you want to know exactly what makes him tick, just read on!

APPEARANCE

Girls aren't the only ones who are obsessed by their appearance — boys are, too! As they reach adolescence, boys are only too aware of the way they look.

They worry about whether they're muscular or puny, whether they've got anything resembling a beard or not, and whether their voices have broken or not. Even in these days of equality, there's still a lot of pressure on boys to be big and strong and "manly."

So stop and think how sensitive and anxious a boy is likely to be if he's small, or skinny, or a late developer. It might help you understand him a bit better!

BRAGGING

Most boys boast a lot — they can't help it. They boast about their bikes, motor bikes, stereos and girls. Boys together have a bad influence on one another — well, they certainly often feel pressurised by their mates into pretending that they're doing things that they're actually miles away from experiencing.

So beware if you hear a boy boasting about his success with girls. Don't jump to the conclusion that a girl's "easy" just because you overhear a boy saying so (especially if you hear a boy saying so!).

COMMITMENT

Many boys are afraid of having a really deep relationship with a girl. Younger boys want to go out with their mates and they usually only want to see a girl now and then (while still being able to boast that they've got a girlfriend). Older boys like to play the field. There are some boys who aren't afraid of committing themselves, but they're unusual.

DOUBLE STANDARDS

For hundreds of years the Double Standard has ruled — and ruined —

women's lives. It means that men feel it's all right for them to have lots of girls, but not for girls to have a lot of boyfriends. They also want one special girlfriend or wife — and if _she_ goes around with other men, that's unforgivable!

This crazy (and unfair) notion is dying out, but there are still boys around who demand faithfulness from their girlfriends whilst happily two-timing them themselves.

FIGHTING

When boys are little, fighting is never taken seriously. Sometimes, mothers and fathers encourage it! But when boys grow up they fight because it's difficult to control their anger at a time when all their emotions are much stronger than before. Also, a lot of boys fight because it makes them look big — or at least they *think* it does.

GANGS

Most boys want to be in some sort of gang. When they are in a gang, there's a lot of pressure on each individual to behave only in ways which are acceptable to the gang. This might include aggro at football matches, boasting about their sexual experiences, or getting drunk. Most boys won't like doing a lot of the things that the gang says he must, but it takes a really strong character to stand out against it and refuse to take part.

IMMATURITY

Most girls find that boys their own age are a bit immature. This is because girls mature, physically and emotionally, a couple of years earlier than boys. A girl of thirteen or fourteen, for example, will find that boys her own age are not only pretty childish but actually more physically immature than her as well.

Most girls therefore tend to go for older boys, until the late teens, when things tend to even out.

KISSING

Everybody's interested in kissing. In general, though, boys don't have the same kind of approach to it as girls do. A girl's likely to get interested in a boy first and _then_ want to kiss him. A boy is more likely to want to kiss a girl — _any_ girl — just to see what it's like.

A kiss may mean very different things to the two people involved. You might be crazy about him, but he may be just experimenting. So beware!

BOY FACTS!

LOVE

People need to feel loved to be happy and secure, but boys especially are often scared of admitting this. They feel that if they say they love their girlfriends, they'll be trapped. The last thing they want is for their mates to think that they're under a girl's thumb. So even a boy who does love you may not admit it — even to himself.

OPENNESS

Complete honesty in relationships is worth working for, but with boys you really will have to work for it. For a start, most boys are afraid of hurting girls so they tell them what they think they want to hear, not what's really true.

Your boyfriend might tell you you look great even when you know your new dress doesn't suit you. And he'll tell you he never looks at other girls when you know he does.

Total honesty really is the best basis for a relationship, though — then, you're likely to stay friends whatever happens!

PUBS

Drinking is one thing boys all seem to think is masculine. Lots of boys get drunk at parties and go to pubs when they're under-age just to prove how tough they are. Unfortunately, there's nothing that looks worse or less appealing than a drunk!

If your guy shows signs of thinking that drinking is something big, tell him in no uncertain terms just how stupid you think drunks are — boring and unsexy. Then, maybe he'll think twice before trying to prove himself in such a daft way!

QUESTIONS

He doesn't know much about you and you don't know much about him, right? Well, it makes sense for you to ask each other questions, especially about sex, love and marriage and your attitudes to them.

ROMANCE

Romance is all about the excitement which surrounds getting to know someone of the opposite sex, being attracted to them and becoming fascinated by them.

The thing to remember, though, is that a boy will enjoy things in private with you that he'd never, ever dream of admitting to when he's with his mates. So show some tact and don't remind him of romantic things he's done and said, especially when he's with a gang of his toughest mates!

TENDERNESS

Most girls need tenderness from their boyfriends, but some boys are reluctant to give it. It's not that they don't feel it: they get embarrassed and shy.

You may have to teach your boyfriend to be affectionate, but don't despair — it *can* be done!

UGLY HABITS

Lots of boys act in some pretty terrible (disgusting!) ways when they're with other boys. Some of them think it impresses girls. Things like dirty talk, filthy jokes and constant swearing aren't a sign that your boyfriend is a yob, though.

It might just be that he's trying to impress you. If it doesn't impress you (and it shouldn't!) tell him so.

WOLFS

Sooner or later, you're going to meet a *wolf* — a boy with wandering hands. If he's a stranger and you're enjoying a slow dance with him at the disco when he suddenly starts to grope you, then you should just break away from him. You don't have to make a big scene about it — just be firm.

If your steady boyfriend starts to get a bit much, though, that's different: he's probably getting carried away by his feelings for you as well as seeing how far he can get! Now is the time to have a serious talk about where to draw the line. Make sure you draw the line where *you* want it.

YOUNGER BOYS

Don't write off younger boys (that is, boys of your own age) as possible boyfriends. They may be smaller than you and more immature, but the nice thing about them is that they're likely to be mates with you first, and then, as they grow up, change into something more.

Younger boys are more likely to treat you with the respect you deserve than some older boys who like to prove how grown-up and powerful they are by treating you like a child.

ZZZzzz . . .

A lot of boys are boring and are more likely to send you to sleep than to set your heart racing. Unfortunately, a lot of girls put up with boys like this because they think having a boyfriend (even a boring one) is better than not having a boyfriend at all.

Well, that's rubbish — and one sure way of putting you off other boyfriends for life!

please don't smoke

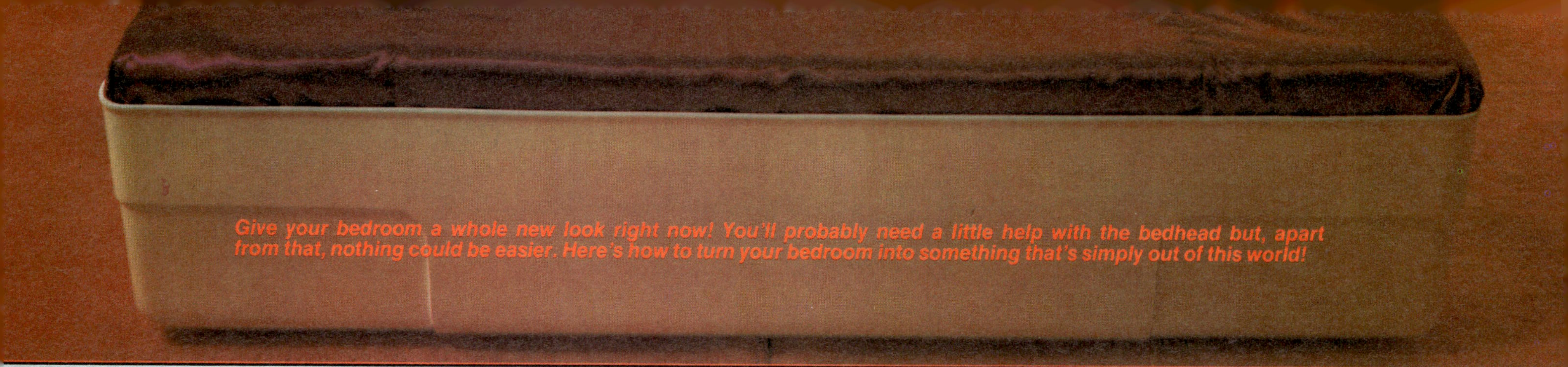

MAKE ROOM FOR THIS!

OVER ALL

The complete headboard design can be painted straight on to the wall, or the girl can be cut from plywood, painted and then fixed to the wall with large picture hooks.

If you have a plain bedspread, liven it up with something along the lines of this "please don't smoke" appliqué design. If you don't have one, start afresh with some silky curtain fabric, or a satin-look sheet. Depending on the type of bed you have, the bedspread can be made to fit a box-type divan, as in our picture, or can simply be a floor-length throw-over. Either way, the result will be sensational!

THE WALL

For painting the wall, you'll need Cover Plus paints (available from Woolworths), as follows:

Stars – Kingfisher (matt vinyl)
Girl – Powder Pink, Sand Gold (silk vinyl) Tangerine, Geranium, Morocco (matt vinyl)

Draw the girl on to the wall and paint, allowing each colour to become touch-dry before painting on the next. When completely dry, you could stick paper stars on to the bathing suit. Rub out any pencil lines still showing.

THE BEDHEAD

If you have help at hand, the bedhead can be made from plywood.

To make the bedhead from plywood, you'll need:

13 mm plywood 900 mm deep x 1050 mm wide (single bed)
(900 mm X 1066 mm for a double bed)
Cover Plus gloss paints for the girl in colours similar to those above
2 wall plugs
2 large picture hooks and eyes

Draw the girl on to the plywood and cut out the shape with a small saw. Paint as above, using gloss paint. When dry, decorate the bathing suit with stars. Fix the picture "eyes" to the back, drill two corresponding holes in the wall above the bed, insert the wall plugs and large picture hooks and hang the bedhead in place.

THE STARS

Make a template for the five-pointed star.

Tie a pencil to a 103-cm length of string and secure the other end to the bed at the middle of the top edge with a drawing pin. You may need someone to hold it in place.

Keeping the string taut, lightly draw a semi-circle on the wall above the bed. Position the star template at the centre of the arc and pencil round it. Fill in the rest of the stars, working out from this central point. Paint Kingfisher.

THE BEDSPREAD

To appliqué the bedspread, use similar fabrics throughout for a professional finish. You will need materials as follows:

50 cm of 90-cm wide red fabric
20 cm of 90-cm wide white fabric
20 cm of 90-cm wide grey fabric
1 m of 90-cm wide iron-on Vilene
Matching cottons
Dressmaker's coloured chalk and pins
Dylon alphabet transfers or letters collected from newspaper head-lines

INSTRUCTIONS

Iron a 50 cm x 33 cm piece of Vilene on to the wrong side of the red fabric. Draw the lips 47 cm wide x 31 cm deep, on to the Vilene with coloured chalk and cut out the shape. The iron-on Vilene not only stiffens the shape but seals the fabric, preventing fraying. Position the lips, right-side up, on the bedspread, pin, and tack into place.

Cut an 18-cm square of Vilene, iron it on to the back of the grey fabric and cut out the cigarette ash, 15 cm wide and rounding off one end. Iron the remaining Vilene on to the white fabric. Cut a strip 38 cm long x 15 cm wide for the cigarette, and a narrow strip 2.54 cm wide widening to 5 cm at one end x 38 cm long for the gloss on the lips. Pin and tack into position and add on the cigarette ash.

Iron the alphabet transfers on to the Vilene, or draw round the letters cut from newspapers, and cut out the fabric. Draw a chalk semi-circle on to the bedspread above the lips (using a length of string tied to the chalk) and tack the letters in position.

Sew on the appliqué with an ordinary machine stitch, or zig-zag stitch, or hand sew to the bedspread with stab-stitch by bringing the needle up through both fabrics just inside the edge of the shape, and taking the needle down through the bedspread just outside the edge of the shape. Remove tacking and press.

MADGE and BERYL
WHERE ARE YOU GOING, BERYL?
I'M CLEARING OUT THE ATTIC FOR YOUR MOTHER, MADGE
I'LL COME TOO!
IT CERTAINLY NEEDS SORTING OUT!
I'LL ORGANISE A LITTLE JUMBLE SALE—DO YOU WANT TO HELP?
YES, PLEASE!
WE'LL DIVIDE EVERYTHING INTO GROUPS
BRIC A BRAC GOES INTO THIS BOX
CHILDRENS' CLOTHES IN HERE AND ADULTS IN HERE
SHALL I PRICE THINGS AS WE GO?
YES-I SUPPOSE SO..
THESE BOOKS LOOK TO BE WORTH A BIT!
THIS FUR COAT SHOULD BRING IN A LOT
I'LL PRICE A FEW THINGS CHEAPLY-THE PUNTERS LIKE A BARGAIN!
WE MUST CHARGE A HIGH ENTRANCE FEE -WE DON'T WANT ANY RIFF RAFF
..AND WE SHOULD HAVE A TABLE FOR CREDIT CARD SALES
NOW, WHERE SHOULD WE HOLD IT? A POSH HOTEL WOULD BE NICE
MALCOLM BIRD
WE COULD INVITE A FILM STAR TO OPEN IT
IT'S THE ONLY WAY—SHE'D HAVE CHARGED FOR HER HELP NEXT!
CONSULTANCY FEE
VAT
TOTAL

YOUR DOTTY DREAMS AND WHAT THEY MEAN!

What sort of dreams do *you* have? Are they pretty ordinary or simply weird, wonderful and way out? Whatever you dream about, you can bet your boots there's a meaning behind it. Wise up on the meaning of your dreams with us right now!

BEAR Dream of a lovely, tame, cuddly teddy type bear and it shows you're longing for someone who's gentle and strong, someone who'll soak up your tears and never growl even if you squeeze him too hard. On the other hand, a *wild* bear means that someone's out to get you and you'd be well advised to flee the country or invest in a pair of dark glasses. Preferably both.

CAT Dreaming of a cat with CLAWS and FANGS is a sure sign that someone somewhere is just dying to get her claws into you. Your subconscious mind is trying to give you a warning to make yourself scarcer than a hair on Elton John's head.

DINOSAUR You're in love with your English teacher who's at least 25 if he's a day. Dreaming of dinosaurs obviously means that you're heavily into prehistoric monsters — or older men, as they're sometimes known. But watch your step because dinosaurs can be tricky customers (even if they do drive nice cars and know how to treat a cave-woman).

FRISBEE In this dream, you might be playing with a Frisbee in the park (or you might actually *be* the Frisbee)! This is a very fantastic dream, showing that you're very probably off your head. If this isn't in fact the case, you're probably a real high flyer. In fact, as far as you're concerned, the sky's the limit.

GIANT If you're the giant, and everybody else is scurrying about like little ants — well, it means you're either terribly worried about being over 6 feet tall or you're a bit of a big head. If, in the dream, you actually hate being so big then it means you need to go on a diet.

KANGAROO Dreaming about a kangaroo could mean that you've got a crush on an Australian. But if the kangaroo is bounding about, it's a pretty sure sign that you're HOPPING mad about something.

LOVE LETTER Dream of receiving a love letter from you-know-who, swooning and clasping it to your heart, and it means you're obviously madly in love, you fool! In fact, you're probably *too* much in love for your own good, though it's a fat lot of good trying to tell you *that*.

NOSES Not many people dream of noses so you're obviously a very unusual person. If you dream you've got a pain in your nose, it probably means your teddy bear's got his paw stuck in it.

PARTY If the party is a good one, and you're having a great time, dancing with Bill Thrill and in general behaving disgracefully, it shows that you're a real swinger. If the party's bad, you don't know anybody, you feel stupid, and you're wearing all the wrong things, it means that you're not a swinger.

QUEEN If you dream that you meet the Queen, that she likes you, and then invites you back to the Palace to meet Prince Andrew — well, you're very common. This is the most common dream of all and you're a very unexceptional girl if this is the kind of dream you have.

ROLLERSKATING You're obviously trying to do something that you're not entirely sure about, something that makes you feel insecure and a bit nervous. You're probably going out with a mad biker or a boy who's a tearaway, or you're trying to teach yourself Russian or Chinese Cooking.

STRING Lots and lots of tangly string? What a crystal-clear dream: you obviously have your eye on some poor unsuspecting boy and you just can't *wait* to get HIM on a string.

VEST You dream you're walking down the High Street in your vest, or less? This means that you feel you've been telling your secrets to the wrong person.

WOOD If you dream of being lost and abandoned in a dark wood, then it means you shouldn't go on that holiday to the Black Forest.

You've lost your way somewhere along the line — maybe you're taking lots of exams in Home Economics when what you really want is to be a tight-rope walker?

X-RAY EYES You can see through everything: you can even tell what colour your Uncle Stan's underpants are (*if* you dream in colour, that is). What a wonderful dream! Or is it? What it means is that you feel very confident, as if you can handle anything — even one of Aunt Edna's rock cakes.

ZOO You're in the zoo, and lots of strange animals are eyeing you up (well, makes a change from the boy-next-door). You feel fascinated but a bit uncertain. This dream means you're aware of how fast you're growing up and you're getting used to living in an adult world, full of grown-up people and orang-utans (difficult to tell the difference, sometimes).

This Christmas was going to be different—I could feel it in my bones. It wouldn't matter if Pierre came to stay in the flat, because Myrtle and I would be living it up in sunny Rio de Janeiro . . .
TPAOLJWTF LIAWTHSAH
OR
The Pathetic Attempts of Leonard J. Watkins To Find Love In A World That Has Something Against Him.
But I should have known better than to tell Russ about my plan . . .
YOU'RE KIDNAPPING MYRTLE? WHAT DO YOU THINK YOU ARE —A SICILIAN BANDIT?
DON'T BE A FOOL! HER OLD MAN DOESN'T HAVE ANY MONEY. NO—I'M TAKING MYRTLE TO SOUTH AMERICA . . .
WHAT'S SO SPECIAL ABOUT CHRISTMAS IN SOUTH AMERICA?
PIERRE WON'T BE THERE! THAT'S WHAT'S SO SPECIAL ABOUT IT!
EVERY YEAR THAT OILY FROG-LEGGED GIT TURNS UP. HE SLEEPS IN MY BED, EATS MY FOOD . . .
. . . PINCHES YOUR GIRL!
THAT'S WHY I'VE GOT TO TAKE MYRTLE TO RIO. JUST THINK—THE SWAYING PALMS, THE STRUMMING OF GUITARS, THE TROPICANA COCKTAILS . . .
. . . THE HEAD-HUNTERS, THE MOSQUITOES, THE YELLOW FEVER, THE AIR-FARE . . .
AIR-FARE . . ?
I'D COME ALONG FOR THE RIDE, BUT THERE'S ONLY 23½P IN THE PIGGY BANK . . .
NOT REALLY ENOUGH TO GET US TO RIO, IS IT?
NEVER MIND! IF WE'RE TOO BROKE TO GO ABROAD, MAYBE PIERRE IS, AS WELL!
YOU'RE RIGHT. HE'S TOO WEEDY TO SWIM THE CHANNEL, AND FAR TOO MEAN TO PAY THE FARE . . .
SO HE MIGHT NEVER GET HERE . . .
CHRISTMAS WITHOUT PIERRE! OH, SANTA—YOU GOT MY LETTER! YOU GOT IT!

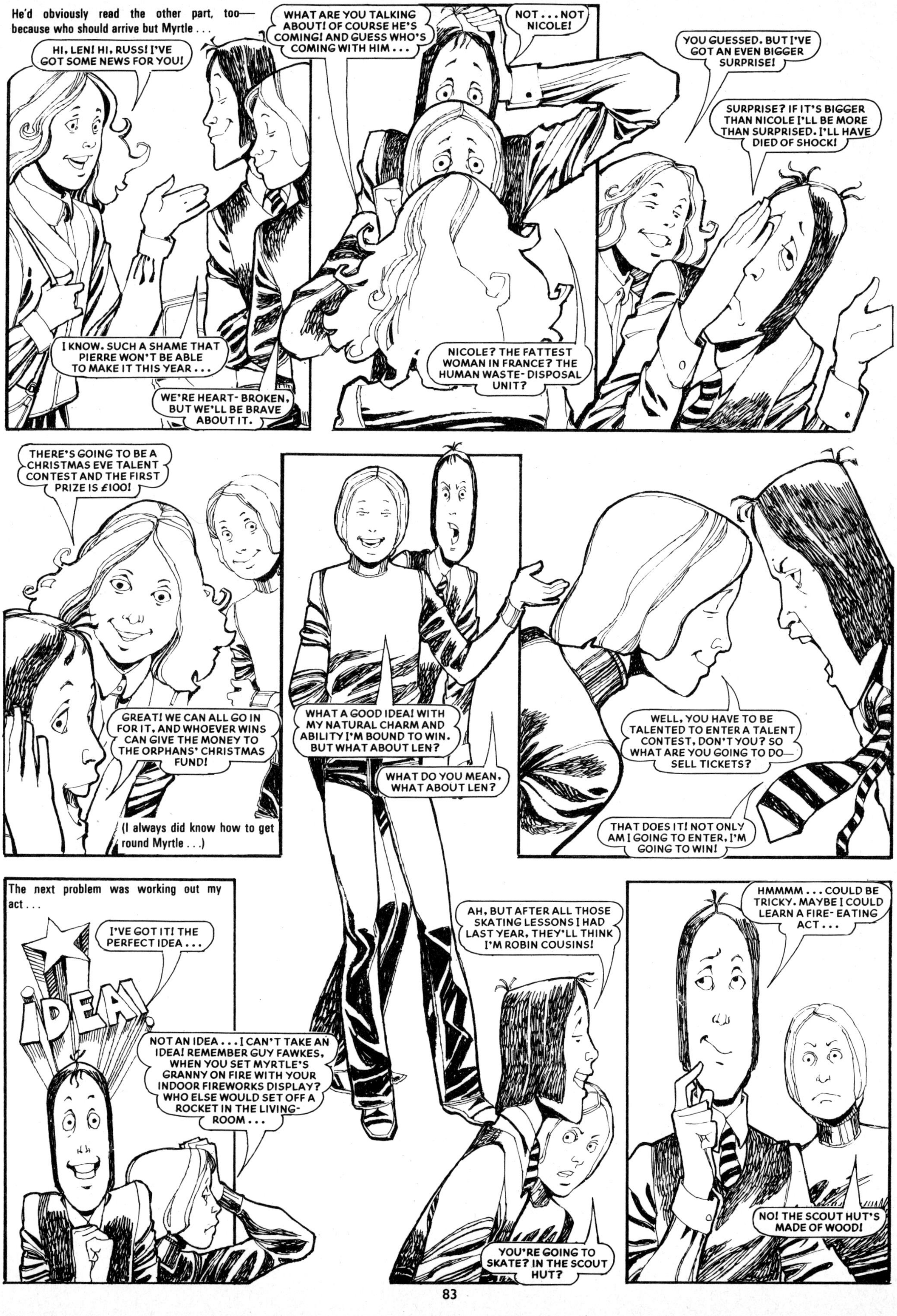
He'd obviously read the other part, too—because who should arrive but Myrtle . . .
HI, LEN! HI, RUSS! I'VE GOT SOME NEWS FOR YOU!
I KNOW. SUCH A SHAME THAT PIERRE WON'T BE ABLE TO MAKE IT THIS YEAR . . .
WE'RE HEART-BROKEN, BUT WE'LL BE BRAVE ABOUT IT.
WHAT ARE YOU TALKING ABOUT! OF COURSE HE'S COMING! AND GUESS WHO'S COMING WITH HIM . . .
NOT . . . NOT NICOLE!
NICOLE? THE FATTEST WOMAN IN FRANCE? THE HUMAN WASTE-DISPOSAL UNIT?
YOU GUESSED. BUT I'VE GOT AN EVEN BIGGER SURPRISE!
SURPRISE? IF IT'S BIGGER THAN NICOLE I'LL BE MORE THAN SURPRISED. I'LL HAVE DIED OF SHOCK!
THERE'S GOING TO BE A CHRISTMAS EVE TALENT CONTEST AND THE FIRST PRIZE IS £100!
GREAT! WE CAN ALL GO IN FOR IT, AND WHOEVER WINS CAN GIVE THE MONEY TO THE ORPHANS' CHRISTMAS FUND!
(I always did know how to get round Myrtle . . .)
WHAT A GOOD IDEA! WITH MY NATURAL CHARM AND ABILITY I'M BOUND TO WIN. BUT WHAT ABOUT LEN?
WHAT DO YOU MEAN, WHAT ABOUT LEN?
WELL, YOU HAVE TO BE TALENTED TO ENTER A TALENT CONTEST, DON'T YOU? SO WHAT ARE YOU GOING TO DO—SELL TICKETS?
THAT DOES IT! NOT ONLY AM I GOING TO ENTER, I'M GOING TO WIN!
The next problem was working out my act . . .
I'VE GOT IT! THE PERFECT IDEA . . .
IDEA!
NOT AN IDEA . . . I CAN'T TAKE AN IDEA! REMEMBER GUY FAWKES, WHEN YOU SET MYRTLE'S GRANNY ON FIRE WITH YOUR INDOOR FIREWORKS DISPLAY? WHO ELSE WOULD SET OFF A ROCKET IN THE LIVING-ROOM . . .
AH, BUT AFTER ALL THOSE SKATING LESSONS I HAD LAST YEAR, THEY'LL THINK I'M ROBIN COUSINS!
YOU'RE GOING TO SKATE? IN THE SCOUT HUT?
HMMMM . . . COULD BE TRICKY. MAYBE I COULD LEARN A FIRE-EATING ACT . . .
NO! THE SCOUT HUT'S MADE OF WOOD!

HOW ABOUT BELLY-DANCING?
I DON'T THINK THE VICAR WOULD BE TOO PLEASED. AND IT MIGHT GIVE MYRTLE SOME FUNNY IDEAS . . .
OK, OK—IF YOU'RE SO SMART, WHAT ARE YOU GOING TO DO?
I THOUGHT I MIGHT SING ALONG WITH MY GUITAR.
BUT YOU'RE GOOD! YOU MIGHT EVEN WIN . . . HOW AM I SUPPOSED TO WIN MYRTLE IF I DON'T WIN THE TALENT CONTEST? YOU'VE GOT TO LOSE, RUSS—THAT'S WHAT FRIENDS ARE FOR.
ALL RIGHT, THEN—JUST TELL ME WHAT YOU WANT ME TO DO . . .
WELL, YOU SEE, IT'S LIKE THIS . . .
Meanwhile . . .
PIERRE! IT'S SO GOOD TO SEE YOU AGAIN!
AH, MYRTLE—I HAVE NOT SPARED THE EXPENSE IN COMING TO SEE YOU. MY UNCLE'S ONION LORRY TOOK US ONLY TO THE NEXT TOWN, SO WE HAVE SPENT 40 PENCE FOR THE BUS!
WE ARE FAINT WITH HUNGER. WHERE IS THE FOOD?
I might have known that French git would be interested in the hundred quid!
BUT FOR THE MAN OF MY TALENTS, THIS CONTEST WILL BE MONEY FOR THE JAM!
AH, THE JAM! IT IS MADE OF THE STRAW-BERRIES?
WE WILL SING TOGETHER THE LOVE DUETS. THEY WILL NOT BE RESISTING OF US.
OH, PIERRE—WHAT A LOVELY IDEA! YOU'RE SO ROMANTIC . . .
MAKES YOU SICK JUST LISTENING TO HIM!
MAKES YOU SICK JUST WATCHING HER!
THE GIRLS, THEY WILL GO WILD AT MY HANDSOME FACE.
I HADN'T THOUGHT OF THAT . . .
AND ME, I WILL DO THE TAP-DANCE!
IN THE SCOUT HUT?
SHE'D BE LUCKY TO FIT INTO THE ALBERT HALL!
. . . AND RUSS IS GOING TO DO HIS MAGIC ACT!
I AM?

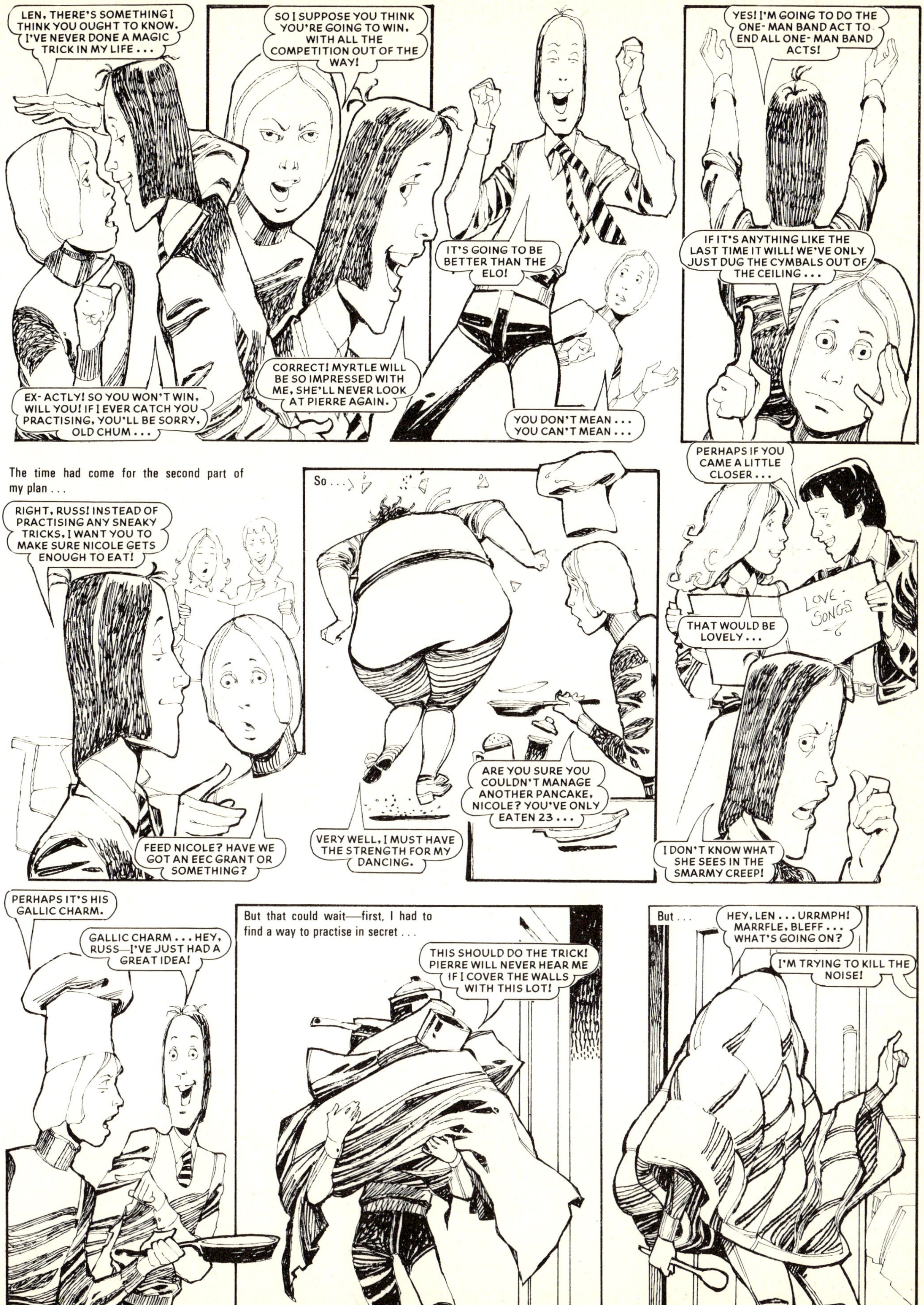
LEN, THERE'S SOMETHING I THINK YOU OUGHT TO KNOW. I'VE NEVER DONE A MAGIC TRICK IN MY LIFE ...
EX-ACTLY! SO YOU WON'T WIN, WILL YOU! IF I EVER CATCH YOU PRACTISING, YOU'LL BE SORRY, OLD CHUM ...
SO I SUPPOSE YOU THINK YOU'RE GOING TO WIN, WITH ALL THE COMPETITION OUT OF THE WAY!
CORRECT! MYRTLE WILL BE SO IMPRESSED WITH ME, SHE'LL NEVER LOOK AT PIERRE AGAIN.
IT'S GOING TO BE BETTER THAN THE ELO!
YOU DON'T MEAN ... YOU CAN'T MEAN ...
YES! I'M GOING TO DO THE ONE-MAN BAND ACT TO END ALL ONE-MAN BAND ACTS!
IF IT'S ANYTHING LIKE THE LAST TIME IT WILL! WE'VE ONLY JUST DUG THE CYMBALS OUT OF THE CEILING ...
The time had come for the second part of my plan ...
RIGHT, RUSS! INSTEAD OF PRACTISING ANY SNEAKY TRICKS, I WANT YOU TO MAKE SURE NICOLE GETS ENOUGH TO EAT!
FEED NICOLE? HAVE WE GOT AN EEC GRANT OR SOMETHING?
So ...
VERY WELL, I MUST HAVE THE STRENGTH FOR MY DANCING.
ARE YOU SURE YOU COULDN'T MANAGE ANOTHER PANCAKE, NICOLE? YOU'VE ONLY EATEN 23 ...
PERHAPS IF YOU CAME A LITTLE CLOSER ...
LOVE SONGS
THAT WOULD BE LOVELY ...
I DON'T KNOW WHAT SHE SEES IN THE SMARMY CREEP!
PERHAPS IT'S HIS GALLIC CHARM.
GALLIC CHARM ... HEY, RUSS—I'VE JUST HAD A GREAT IDEA!
But that could wait—first, I had to find a way to practise in secret ...
THIS SHOULD DO THE TRICK! PIERRE WILL NEVER HEAR ME IF I COVER THE WALLS WITH THIS LOT!
But ...
HEY, LEN ... URRMPH! MARRFLE, BLEFF ... WHAT'S GOING ON?
I'M TRYING TO KILL THE NOISE!

YOU NEARLY KILLED ME! ANYWAY, WHY DO YOU HAVE TO USE MY DOWNIE? WHAT'S WRONG WITH YOURS?
IT'S ON MY BED, THAT'S WHAT! ANYWAY, EVERY ARTIST MUST PRACTISE!
WELL, I CAN'T FEED NICOLE WITHOUT POTS AND PANS. YOU'LL HAVE TO PRACTISE SOMEWHERE ELSE?
LIKE WHERE?
WHAT ABOUT THE GARAGE WHERE ALAN WORKS? HE OWES YOU A FAVOUR AFTER YOU BROKE HIS ARM FOR HIM AND GOT HIM THREE MONTHS OFF WORK...
I DON'T KNOW IF HE'LL SEE IT THAT WAY, BUT IT'S WORTH A TRY...
So I practised in the garage, and everyone was happy. Well, almost everyone...
GARAGE
IT MUST BE A POLTERGEIST! NO LIVING CREATURE COULD MAKE SUCH A TERRIBLE NOISE...
Then, the night before the contest I made everyone a very special meal...
WHAT'S THE BIG IDEA! YOU KNOW I CAN'T STAND GARLIC!
YOU SHOULD WORRY! THERE'S FOUR TIMES AS MUCH IN PIERRE'S. HIS TASTE-BUDS ARE SO NUMB WITH ALL THOSE THROAT SPRAYS HE'S BEEN USING TO IMPROVE HIS VOICE, HE'LL NEVER NOTICE!
WHY DO YOU NOT EAT, RUSS? YOU ARE THE FIRST IN THE SHOW TOMORROW, NON?
PHEW! ER... IT MUST HAVE BEEN THE EFFORT OF MAKING THOSE PANCAKES THIS AFTERNOON. I'M TOO SLEEPY TO EAT...
Russ was so exhausted from feeding Nicole non-stop, his act was even better than I'd hoped...
TALENT CONTEST
I'M SURE THERE ARE SIX WHITE DOVES IN HERE SOMEWHERE...
WHAT A LAUGH!
HE'S BETTER THAN TOMMY COOPER ANY DAY!
AND WHEN I OPEN THE CUPBOARD DOOR, HEY PRESTO! A LOVELY WHITE RABBIT!
SOME RABBIT!
SORRY, RUSS. I AM HAVING THE LITTLE SNACK!
LOOKS MORE LIKE AN ELEPHANT TO ME!
And, eventually...
I'M SORRY, FOLKS—THIS ACT IS SO AWFUL I'M SURPRISED YOU HAVEN'T FALLEN ASLEEP. IN FACT, I THINK I'LL JUST HAVE A LITTLE NAP MYSELF. THIS SHOW'S SO BORING...

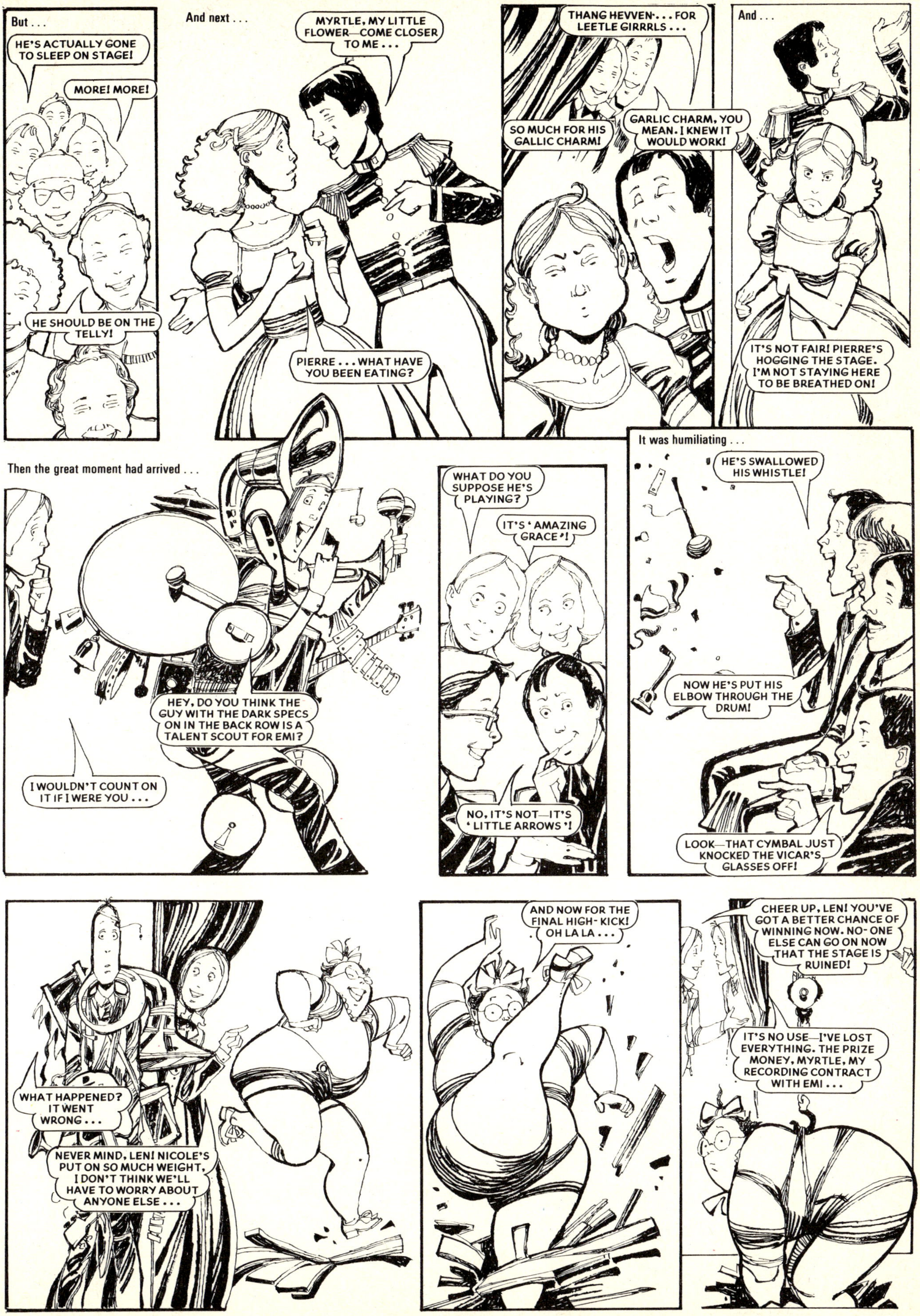

But . . .
HE'S ACTUALLY GONE TO SLEEP ON STAGE!
MORE! MORE!
HE SHOULD BE ON THE TELLY!
And next . . .
MYRTLE, MY LITTLE FLOWER—COME CLOSER TO ME . . .
PIERRE . . . WHAT HAVE YOU BEEN EATING?
THANG HEVVEN . . . FOR LEETLE GIRRRLS . . .
SO MUCH FOR HIS GALLIC CHARM!
GARLIC CHARM, YOU MEAN. I KNEW IT WOULD WORK!
And . . .
IT'S NOT FAIR! PIERRE'S HOGGING THE STAGE. I'M NOT STAYING HERE TO BE BREATHED ON!
Then the great moment had arrived . . .
HEY, DO YOU THINK THE GUY WITH THE DARK SPECS ON IN THE BACK ROW IS A TALENT SCOUT FOR EMI?
I WOULDN'T COUNT ON IT IF I WERE YOU . . .
WHAT DO YOU SUPPOSE HE'S PLAYING?
IT'S 'AMAZING GRACE'!
NO, IT'S NOT—IT'S 'LITTLE ARROWS'!
It was humiliating . . .
HE'S SWALLOWED HIS WHISTLE!
NOW HE'S PUT HIS ELBOW THROUGH THE DRUM!
LOOK—THAT CYMBAL JUST KNOCKED THE VICAR'S GLASSES OFF!
WHAT HAPPENED? IT WENT WRONG . . .
NEVER MIND, LEN! NICOLE'S PUT ON SO MUCH WEIGHT, I DON'T THINK WE'LL HAVE TO WORRY ABOUT ANYONE ELSE . . .
AND NOW FOR THE FINAL HIGH-KICK! OH LA LA . . .
CHEER UP, LEN! YOU'VE GOT A BETTER CHANCE OF WINNING NOW. NO-ONE ELSE CAN GO ON NOW THAT THE STAGE IS RUINED!
IT'S NO USE—I'VE LOST EVERYTHING. THE PRIZE MONEY, MYRTLE, MY RECORDING CONTRACT WITH EMI . . .

But . . .
I'M AFRAID THE REST OF THE CONTEST WILL HAVE TO BE CANCELLED. BUT WE'VE DECIDED TO AWARD THE PRIZE MONEY JOINTLY TO THE TWO COMEDY ACTS.
COMEDY ACTS . . ???
THE FIRST PRIZE GOES TO LEN AND RUSS!
US . . ???
WE'VE WON!!!
NOW WE CAN DONATE THE MONEY TO THE ORPHANS!
THAT'S VERY GENEROUS OF YOU.
OH, LEN—YOU'RE GIVING THE MONEY TO THE POOR ORPHANS! YOU'RE WONDERFUL, YOU REALLY ARE!
IT WAS NOTHING, MYRTLE! REALLY . . .
THIS IS THE OUTRAGE! HE CANNOT WIN! I WAS THE BEST —AND I NEED THE MONEY FOR MY NEW STEREO EQUIPMENT!
YOU WERE GOING TO KEEP THE MONEY FOR YOURSELF ALL THE TIME! YOU NEVER MEANT TO GIVE IT TO THE POOR ORPHANS!
THE STUPID ORPHANS ARE POOR, BUT I AM POOR, TOO! THE FRENCH ARE NOT SO STUPID AS YOU ENGLISH . . .
OH, LEONARD—I'M SO GLAD I FOUND OUT WHAT HE'S REALLY LIKE! YOU'RE SO KIND AND GENEROUS . . .
TRUE, QUITE TRUE . . .
IN FACT, I WAS GOING TO TAKE YOU TO RIO FOR A SURPRISE, BUT IF I BORROW A FIVER FROM RUSS WE COULD GO TO THAT NEW LATIN AMERICAN CLUB . . .
OH, LEN—THIS IS THE BEST CHRISTMAS EVER!
YOU'RE RIGHT, MYRTLE. YOU'RE ABSOLUTELY RIGHT!
THE END

CAN *YOU* TAKE A HINT? WHEN SOMEONE'S TRYING TO TELL YOU SOMETHING BUT IS TOO SHY, POLITE OR EMBARRASSED TO COME RIGHT OUT WITH IT — DO YOU CATCH ON? OR DO SUBTLE HINTS PASS YOU BY? IF THEY DO, LIFE COULD BE A BIT AWKWARD FOR YOU — AND YOUR MATES!

Do You Know When To Take A Hint?

IF your friends start arriving at your house with clothes pegs on their noses, think twice before shouting, "Oh, is that the latest fashion? I must rush out and buy a clothes peg!" Clothes pegs on noses aren't one bit fashionable. Could it be that your friends are trying to tell you something? Is it possible you may have B.O.? (Hadn't thought of that, had you?)

When hints are being dropped, the sooner you catch on — the better. It can save an awful lot of discomfort, especially in the case of B.O., and save your friends from having to buy gas-masks in a desperate last attempt to let you know what's wrong.

Another example is when you're happy and you want to share your happiness. That's understandable. But if you've just started dating The Most Gorgeous Guy In Town, your friends are going to want to know all about him and you're certainly going to tell them.

But, if you keep harping on about it, pretty soon your friends are going to get fed up with hearing about Him (especially if they haven't got boys of their own at the time).

If they start changing the subject every time you mention Him, take the hint. They'll talk about fashion, records, the possibility of life on other planets, and Einstein's Theory of Relativity. Anything except HIM.

If this happens, you should really ease up on talking about Him. Otherwise, in the end, they'll start screaming and tearing out their hair with cries of, "I can't stand any more!"

But what happens when your romance with HIM starts to fade – how is he going to let you know if you're still madly in love with him and haven't noticed him cooling off?

He could come straight out and tell you, but if he doesn't want to hurt your feelings he won't do it like that.

He'll try to be kind about it. That's when hints will start dropping like rocks.

He may leave a note for you saying, *Sorry, can't keep our date tonight. Have emigrated to North Borneo.* This should give you an inkling that he might be cooling off!

But it's more likely he'll be less obvious than that. He'll start breaking dates with weak excuses you don't really believe.

When love's flown out the window it doesn't come back. Take the hints and retire gracefully before he has to resort to more drastic measures, like putting a barbed-wire fence all round his house so you can't drop in to ask why he didn't turn up for your last date.

Don't be the Piggy in the Middle, either. Sometimes, when two girls have been close friends for a long time, one of them still expects their regular meetings to continue even though the other one's got a steady boyfriend and would really like to spend some time alone with him.

If *you're* the one who tags along, keep your eyes open for warning signs. Your friend may not mind you turning up and making a threesome from time to time.

But if you find yourself chatting away about the weather and whether the Bee Gees would look any different if they had the Osmonds' teeth, and your buddy and her guy don't seem to be paying much attention 'cos they're busy cuddling – take the hint.

Even if you ask your friend if she minds if you tag along it doesn't follow that she means no when she says no.

If she doesn't sound as if she means it — that's the hint.

Hints are very indirect. When you've set your mind on buying a particular dress and your friend says: *Are you sure it will suit you?* What she *really* means is, *I don't think it will suit you.*

When you've planned a great scheme of some kind and your enthusiasm is met with a remark like, *Well, yes, I suppose it might be a good idea,* you can be pretty sure your scheme will be a dead loss.

A remark like, *Are you sure you know what you're doing?* is very often a hint that the speaker thinks you don't. If you're a non-swimmer and you're about to jump into the deep end of the swimming pool by mistake, it could turn out to be the last hint you'll ever have a chance to ignore.

Most hints are gentle and well meaning. Some can be cruel or unkind. When you find yourself having to drop hints to let a friend know she's being a pain in the neck in some way, try to do it without hurting her feelings.

If your boyfriend is still hanging around when the lovelight has gone out of your eyes, if your best friend has B.O. or is boring you to tears, make your hints as delicate as you can.

And try to avoid such unsubtle hints as clothes pegs on your nose, barbed-wire fences round your house or running around screaming, *I can't stand any more.*

There are better ways. Anyway, barbed wire is pretty expensive stuff.

SOMETHING BORROWED...

SHAKIN' STEVENS. Elvis Presley lives on — in the shape of Shakin' Stevens.

How Presley's fans feel about the man, we're not too sure, but Shakin' is certainly cashing in on the King's recipe for success. Not only does the slick-haired singer copy Elvis's clothes, he sounds like him and even has Elvis's gyrations duplicated jerk for jerk.

His dark looks have made him a hit with male and female fans alike, and we suppose that as long as there's a market for the Presley-style sound there will be people like Shakin' popping up in the charts.

TOYAH. We bet a lot of you had forgotten all about Lene Lovich till Toyah came along. She sounds so like the Lene, who had super hits with "Lucky Number" and "Say When," that's it's uncanny.

Toyah definitely doesn't *look* like Lene, but listen to her vocals and we're sure you'll find more than a passing resemblance to Lene's style of performing. Something else the two ladies have in common is that they've both been the subject of TV documentaries — an honour reserved for the chosen few.

After Lene's was screened however, the lady just didn't seem able to top her initial success. Toyah, take note!

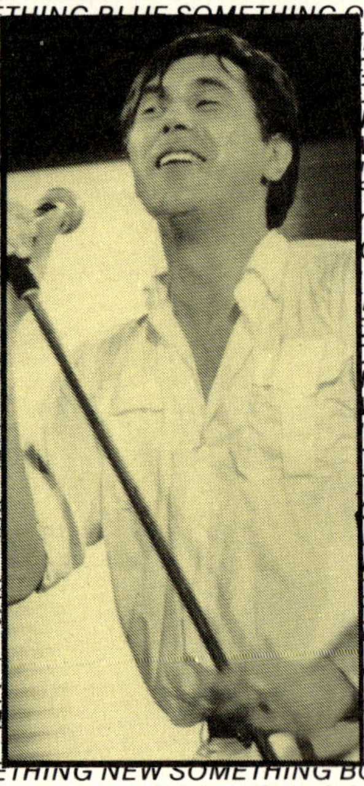

GARY NUMAN. Listening to some of Gary's music is like hearing David Bowie on an "off" day. But, let's be fair to Gary. At least, unlike some artistes, Gary admits that he's been greatly influenced by Bowie. Though we think it goes a bit deeper than that.

It's a pity,however,that Gary has been unable to take a leaf from David's book on learning to cope with success. Perhaps then he'd still be touring and letting his fans hear his music first hand — after all, there's no substitute for the real thing.

BRYAN FERRY. Among the things Bryan has "borrowed" from other performers is a repertoire of classic, standard hits to which he's added his magical touch.

Perhaps the most famous tunes that have the Ferry treatment are Bob Dylan's "A Hard Rain's A-Gonna Fall" and "Smoke Gets In Your Eyes" that was first a hit for The Platters in 1959!

But we don't mind what he pinches because he does everything so well we bet he could make the National Anthem into a top ten hit!

SOMETHING BLUE

LES MCKEOWN. When Les released his album "All Washed Up," he said he'd chosen the title to prove to his critics that he wasn't! The album however didn't do all that well and Les took to ligging around on the other side of the Atlantic with Britt Ekland. So, what's the star, who was once part of The Bay City Rollers, been up to?

Well, things just haven't worked out for Les without the rest of the band. They're all living it up in America and enjoying some success with the American teen market — they always were a few years behind their British counterparts.

Meanwhile, though, Les certainly looks as though he's well and truly — washed up . . .

SMOKEY. Though the band still seem to be popular in Germany, things don't seem to be happening for them in Britain.

Smokey have, however, had their fair share of success since their first hit "If You Think You Know How To Love Me" back in 1975.

Perhaps the punk movement was in some way responsible for the band's demise. Certainly it shook up the record industry and gave it a much-needed spring clean, and since then the band seem to have disappeared in a puff of smoke . . .

THE OSMONDS. The Osmonds have just one thing going for them — their teeth — because they help the incredibly rich performers to keep smiling despite the fact that they're no longer teeny idols.

The Osmonds success seems to have waned since the boys started to get married. Not that we're blaming their wives for the decline, but it now looks as though the family are much too content sitting around at home to go out on the road.

Maybe they're busy working on a second generation group — what a thought!

LEIF GARRETT. Leif is one of those unfortunate people who's been made into a star for no apparent reason. He fits in with the American picture of the good-looking, young blond-haired guy they go wild for. Leif unfortunately doesn't seem to have the talent to go with all the hype.

We're not denying that Leif is a really nice guy — he is — but apart from good looks and nice personality he has nothing. His main ambition is to be taken seriously as a rock singer, but so far all his records have flopped dismally.

The best advice we can give him is to hang on to his skateboard — maybe someone will remember him for that!

YOU KNOW YOU'VE GOT A

YOU KNOW YOU'VE GOT A LOT TO LEARN ABOUT YOUR BOYFRIEND WHEN . . .

. . . each time he gets angry he turns sort of green and all his clothes rip off.

. . . he's got blond hair, plays in a rock group, is called Gordon and is just about to tell you his nick-name . . .

. . . he takes you home to meet his folks and his mum's wearing a tiara and there are these corgis all over the place.

. . . he thinks Cordon Bleu is a striker for Manchester United.

. . . every girl you meet can tell you more about him than you know . . .

. . . he has all these files marked, Top Secret — M15.

. . . every time he takes you out, millions of people start chanting his name and asking for his autograph.

. . . you never see him during the daylight hours, but he's tall, dark and handsome . . . except for those funny little fangs.

. . . he keeps jumping into phone boxes and changing into a blue body stocking and red trunks — then he disappears.

YOU KNOW YOU'VE GOT A LOT TO LEARN WHEN . . .

. . . your exam results arrive in a brown envelope with a slip of paper inside saying, "Was this some kind of joke?"

. . . your class all use a calculator in maths, but you're still having trouble operating the On/Off switch.

. . . you discover that The Birds And The Bees is *not* a Hitchcock thriller.

. . . your dad's phone bill is £150, but you thought the calls were free when you couldn't find the slot to put the money in . . . !

. . . your dad buys you a full set of Encyclopaedia Brittanica and you wonder how the information about a little island like Britain can fill up all those pages . . .

. . . your mum asks you to whip up an omelette for tea, and finds you in the kitchen viciously lashing at an egg with a shoelace.

YOU KNOW YOU'VE GOT A LOT TO LEARN ABOUT YOUR BEST FRIEND WHEN . . .

. . . everyone keeps saying to you, "With a best friend like that, who needs enemies!"

. . . she's always suggesting you borrow her clothes — but she's a size 8 and you're a 16.

. . . she insists you dye your hair blonde and then reveals the guy you fancy only goes for redheads!

. . . every guilty secret you share with her ends up posted on the school notice board.

. . . you find this little wax figure full of pins in her room and it looks remarkably like you!

. . . every time you're not in her company your ears start to burn.

. . . she looks like Kate Bush and you look like the Hunchback of Notre Dame!

. . . her main topic of conversation is *your* boyfriend.

. . . you keep receiving poison pen letters and they're in her handwriting!

LOT TO LEARN WHEN. . .

YOU KNOW YOU'VE GOT A LOT TO LEARN ABOUT SCHOOL WHEN . .

. . . you really think you can do no work and get away with it.

. . . you can't understand why your teachers keep putting kisses all over your work.

. . . you still look forward to school dinners, hoping it's something nice . . .

. . . you're twenty and still in first year!

. . . each time the bell rings you jump up and start shouting "Fire!"

. . . you imagine the writing on your forged absentee note is anything like your mum's.

. . . you think it's the ideal place to meet your friends and have a gossip.

. . . you think a trip to the Careers Officer means seeing someone who'll organise it for you to become a pop star.

. . . you get sent to see the Head and you're looking for this disembodied being!

. . . after three years of French, all you can say is, "Pardon?" in a half-baked French accent.

YOU KNOW YOU'VE GOT A LOT TO LEARN ABOUT MUSIC WHEN . . .

. . . you always thought if anyone was into heavy metal, it meant they worked in the steel industry.

. . . you assumed Police albums were books of criminal photographs.

. . . your boyfriend says he wants to watch "The Old Grey Whistle Test," but you're not interested in freezing to death watching a load of trains whistling through a station.

. . . you think Siouxsie and the Banshees is an Indian tribe.

. . . you search all the record shops for the latest album by The Sweet, and wonder why all the assistants laugh at you.

. . . you think that Mike Stand is a boy who lives down the road.

. . . you think that Orchestral Manoeuvres in the Dark was a concert given by the London Philharmonic during a power cut.

. . . you think they give you two speakers for your stereo in case one breaks down.

. . . you're still waiting for Donny Osmond to ask you to marry him!

. . . you refuse to let your sister put up her Adam and the Ants poster because you don't fancy waking up to a load of insects staring down at you.

. . . you thought Christian Dior was the entrance to a church.

. . . you think that lipstick is what happens when your brother puts glue on your toothbrush.

. . . you think boutiques are something people knit to keep babies' feet warm.

YOU KNOW YOU'VE GOT A LOT TO LEARN ABOUT FASHION WHEN . . .

. . . you dress just as the Jackie fashion pages show you — but the Jackies are your sister's hand-downs dated 1977.

. . . you get all dolled up for the disco and the doorman tells you that "Seventies Night" isn't until next week.

. . . you always thought Levi Strauss composed waltzes.

. . . you've only just started wearing platform shoes after spending years thinking they were only issued to British Rail porters.

. . . you're horrified to see your friend wearing a skirt that's split at the bottom, and even more horrified when she refuses to sew it up!

FOR STAR

LIBRA

(Sept. 22-Oct. 22)

The great romantic, nothing appeals to you like the thought of a candlelit dinner in a lovely restaurant with your boyfriend. You have a very delicate, refined nature, reflected in your tastes in food. You prefer light, attractively-served meals to a great pile of mush and chips. However, you're very easily influenced by others so if your friends decide on hamburger and chips in the Wimpy, you'll go along with them.

You're probably not all that keen on cooking, you'd rather others did it for you. But you'd go all out and do your very best to provide something really nice if you were cooking. A blow-out meal isn't really in your nature — you're too refined — but go on — it's good for you once in a while!

BLOW-OUT MEAL

Spanish pork and rice

Coat slices of pork fillet with flour.
Fry an onion in butter till golden, then add the pork and fry till browned.
Put in casserole.
Fry a green pepper and some mushrooms till tender, and add a can of tomatoes.
Add to meat in casserole, season and cook in medium oven for 1½ hours.
Serve with boiled rice.

SCORPIO

(Oct. 23-Nov. 21)

The Scorpio is fiery and passionate about everything in life, with a determined sense of purpose about her. Pretty secretive, too, so you would probably enjoy surprising people with a fiery meal with unidentifiable bits in it!

Food is exciting to you — you'll try anything (once!) and you really get a kick out of eating. You don't have much of a weight problem as you work off all your energy with physical activity, thereby keeping your size within reasonable limits.

BLOW-OUT MEAL

Curried mince and rice

Fry an onion, green pepper and apple until brown.
Put aside. To fat remaining in pan, add a level tablespoonful curry powder, the same of flour, and cook for two minutes.
Add ½ pint stock or water, bring to boil.
Stir in chutney and sultanas, cook for twenty minutes.
Add already-browned mince, simmer for half an hour.
Serve with boiled rice.

SAGITTARIUS

(Nov. 22-Dec. 21)

You need a great deal of physical exercise, and if you're ever tired it's usually through boredom. So health-giving, energy foods are high on the list for you. You're very body conscious, so you hate stodgy foods which leave you bloated.

You're very happy, so eating should be fun for you, and versatility and adaptability are two of your strong characteristics so you can whip a meal up anywhere, anytime.

You love the idea of an open-air picnic in the country, with plenty of space, and good, wholesome, country-style food. You're very aware of the fact that you are what you eat, and, if not already vegetarian, you give the matter a lot of thought.

BLOW-OUT MEAL

Ratatouille

Heat two tablespoonfuls butter and ½ oz. oil in casserole and add two large onions, peeled and chopped; one large aubergine, chopped; one green or red pepper, chopped; four tomatoes, skinned and chopped; four courgettes, sliced; one clove garlic, crushed; two level tblspns. tomato paste; chopped parsley, salt, pepper. Cover and put in medium oven for one hour.